THE PRESENCE OF GOD

In His Universe
In His Word
In His Son
In His People
and
Other Sermons

by

Henry Clay Morrison

First Fruits Press
Wilmore, Kentucky
c2012

asburyseminary.edu
800.2ASBURY
204 North Lexington Avenue
Wilmore, Kentucky 40390

ISBN: 9781621710257

The Presence of God in His universe, in His word, in His Son, in His People : and Other Sermons, by Henry Clay Morrison.
First Fruits Press, © 2012
Originally published by the Pentecostal Publishing Company

Digital version at
http://place.asburyseminary.edu/firstfruitsheritagematerial/19

First Fruits Press is a digital imprint of the Asbury Theological Seminary, B.L. Fisher Library. Asbury Theological Seminary is the legal owner of the material previously published by the Pentecostal Publishing Co. and reserves the right to release new editions of this material as well as new material produced by Asbury Theological Seminary. Its publications are available for noncommercial and educational uses, such as research, teaching and private study. First Fruits Press has licensed the digital version of this work under the Creative Commons Attribution Noncommercial 3.0 United States License. To view a copy of this license, visit http://creativecommons.org/licenses/by-nc/3.0/us/.

For all other uses, contact:

First Fruits Press
B.L. Fisher Library
Asbury Theological Seminary
204 N. Lexington Ave.
Wilmore, KY 40390
http://place.asburyseminary.edu/firstfruits

Morrison, H. C. (Henry Clay), 1857-1942
 The presence of God in His universe, in His word, in His Son, in His people : and other sermons / by H.C. Morrison.
 Wilmore, Ky. : First Fruits Press, c2012.
 155 p. ; 21 cm.
 Reprint. Previously published: Louisville, Ky. : Pentecostal Publishing Company, [192-?].
 ISBN: 9781621710257 (pbk.)
 1. Methodist Church – Sermons. 2. Sermons, American. I. Title.
 BX8333 .M6 P7 2012

Cover design by Haley Hill

asburyseminary.edu
800.2ASBURY
204 North Lexington Avenue
Wilmore, Kentucky 40390

THE PRESENCE OF GOD

In His Universe   In His Word
In His Son   In His People

And

OTHER SERMONS

By

Rev. H. C. MORRISON, D. D.

Published by
PENTECOSTAL PUBLISHING COMPANY
LOUISVILLE, KENTUCKY

FOREWORD

During the long months when I was confined to my room by illness and deprived of the privilege of preaching the gospel to the listening multitudes, my mind was busy thinking of the needs of humanity and how fully those needs are met in the Christ who gave Himself so fully and so willingly for the salvation of men.

My thoughts often form themselves into sermon messages. I have put them down in this volume with the hope and prayer that they may prove helpful to those who read them. Through all my suffering my faith was unshaken, and my spirit was restful, trusting constantly in the Christ who is mighty to save to the uttermost.

I commend Him, with His willingness and power to pardon and cleanse from all sin all who come to Him with faith for all He has to give to those who claim Him and trust in Him as Saviour and Lord.

H. C. MORRISON.

CONTENTS

	PAGE
The Deity of Christ	5
The Chastening of the Lord	21
The Presence of God	31
Forgiveness	38
The New Birth	50
The Future Punishment of the Wicked	62
The Searchings of the Lord	75
The Baptism With the Holy Spirit	88
In the Beginning God Created the Heavens and the Earth	102
The Crucifixion	117
Entire Sanctification	133

THE DEITY OF CHRIST.

"That all men should honor the Son, even as they honor the Father. He that honoreth not the Son honoreth not the Father which hath sent him."—John 5:23.

Our Lord Jesus Christ in his teachings always claimed his oneness with God the Father. This, more than any other one thing, enraged the Jews against him. When Jesus said, "I and my Father are one, then the Jews took up stones again to stone him." The word "again" would intimate that this was not the first time that they had been ready to stone Jesus.

In Matthew's account of the trial of Jesus, we read, "And the high priest answered and said unto him, I adjure thee by the living God, that thou tell us whether thou be the Christ, the Son of God. Jesus saith unto him, Thou hast said: nevertheless, I say unto you, Hereafter ye shall see the Son of man sitting on the right hand of power, and coming in the clouds of heaven. Then the high priest rent his clothes, saying, He hath spoken blasphemy; what further need have we of witness? Behold, now we have heard his blasphemy, what think ye? And they answered and said, He is guilty of death." Matt. 26:63-66.

This claim of Christ stirred such anger in the Jews that they not only condemned Him to death, but at once, began to spit upon Him, beat and smite Him with the palms of their hands. It was a shocking scene of cruelty and torture. Within the last half century there has sprung up in the Protestant churches of this nation a number of preachers who have attracted to themselves a large following, who deny the Virgin Birth of Christ; they insist that He performed no miracles; they claim there is no virtue in His death to save from sin. They deny His bodily resurrection and ascent into heaven, or that He sits at the right hand of the Father as an intercessor.

These modernistic teachers are far more in harmony with the spirit and action of the Jews who condemned Jesus to death, and would have killed Him, could they legally have done so, than they are in harmony with the disciples of Christ who wrote the New Testament records of His birth, life, teachings, the miracles He performed, His sacrificial death upon the cross, and glorious resurrection. Yet these modernistic preachers are supported by the church, and the attitude of the church is such that they have prominent appointments, receive large salaries, and are in places of influential leadership, and it may be safely said, they have an utter contempt for pastors and evangelists who preach the plain New Testament gospel which is the power of God unto salvation to every one that believeth.

Strange to say, the church is in such condition that in its officiary and administration these false teachers are permitted to go unrebuked by those who are supposed to have places of administrative officialism and power for the protection and guidance of the church, the purity of her doctrine and the sacredness of the person and saving power of our Lord Christ.

One can but wonder what the second generation of these skeptical preachers will believe and have to offer as a message to the people. We cannot build a church that is sacred, that deserves the reverence and support of the people that is not founded upon the Son of God, the truths He spoke, and the sacrificial death He died upon the cross of Calvary. There is salvation in none other than Jesus, and if Jesus is no more than your modern, skeptical preachers make Him, there is no salvation in Him. What is their objective? What business have they in the pulpit? What message have they for a sinful, broken-hearted world?

Thoughtful philosophers who make no claim to Christ as a Saviour from sin, or that He was in any special sense, the Son of God, have paid the highest tributes to His character and teaching. The historian, Lecky, who was a rationalist, says of Jesus: "In the character and example of Christ is an enduring principle of regeneration." What did Lecky mean? He evidently had no thought of the new birth which Jesus taught Nicodemus in the third chapter of John. Perhaps he meant, if men would live in harmony with tne teachings of Christ and seek to pattern after and, as far as possible, duplicate the character of Christ, it would regenerate society and bring a new social order into the world. And doubtless it would.

Renan, an infidel, says: "The person of Christ is at the highest summit of human greatness." He places Jesus on a pinnacle above all the great men of all the ages, the "highest summit of human greatness."

John Stuart Mill, philosopher and agnostic, says of Jesus, "Everything which is excellent in ethics may be brought within the sayings of Christ without doing violence to language. He is the ideal representative and guide to humanity." This statement of Mill's covers a wide territory of all human affairs.

These are glowing tributes to pay to Christ by thoughtful and reverential philosophers, but they are illogical. Jesus claimed much more for Himself than they claim for Him. If He was not what He claimed to be, He could not be what they claimed for Him. He claimed to be the Son of God, one and equal with the Father. He claimed to have power to forgive sins. He claimed existence with the Father before the world was. If Jesus was any less than what He claimed to be, He was the greatest impostor who has ever appeared among men. His life, teachings, character, the power of His name, and the saving efficacy of His gospel through the centuries, afford ample proof that Jesus was not an impostor but the Son of God, mighty to save to the uttermost. Jesus does not seek the compliments and praise of men. He cares nothing for that. He calls men to come to Him in penitence for their sins and faith for salvation through the atoning merits of His blood shed upon the cross of Calvary.

THE PRESENCE OF GOD

Has the reader ever noticed the "I Am's" of Jesus? "I am the bread of life." John 6:36. "Before Abraham was, I am." John 8:58. "I am the light of the world." John 8:12. "I am the door." John 10:9. "I am the resurrection and the life." John 11:25. "I am the way, the truth and the life." John 15:6. "My Father and I are one." John 10:30. Jesus could have made no higher claims for Himself than we find in these wonderful "I Am's." He called a burdened world to come to Him, with the assuurance that He would give it rest. He asserted that at some future time He would return in glory and sit in judgment with the assembled nations before Him.

There is no middle ground for us to take when we approach the Christ of prophecy, of the disciples and the apostles. We must accept Him at what He claimed to be, and what He promised to do for all who come to Him, or reject Him, as a fanatic and false teacher.

There is another passage to which we call your attention, found in John 14:

21: "He that hath my commandments, and keepeth them, he it is that loveth me: and he that loveth me shall be loved of my Father, and I will love him, and will manifest myself to him." It is possible for all believers to go beyond all human records and testimonials and have a personal experience in which Christ is so manifested that they can know that Jesus is all He claimed to be, and able to save from sin. There is another promise that is very precious to believers, found in John 15:26: "But when the Comforter is come, whom I will send unto you from the Father, even the spirit of truth, which proceedeth from the Father, he shall testify of me." The Holy Spirit becomes an abiding witness to the Deity of Christ, His oneness with the Father, the truthfulness of all His claims, and His mightiness to save

Those men who deny the Godhead of Christ have no right to a place in the Christian Church, much less in the pulpit, disseminating their skeptical views and leading the people away from the truth of the gospel to unbelief and death. These false teachers are well described in 1 John 4:2-6: "Hereby know we the Spirit of God: Every spirit that confesseth that Jesus Christ is come in the flesh is of God: and every spirit that confesseth not that Jesus Christ is come in the flesh is not of God: and this is that spirit of antichrist, whereof ye have heard which should come; and even now already it is in the world. Ye are of God, little children, and have overcome them: because greater is he that is in you, than he that is in the world. They are of the world; therefore, speak they of the world, and the world heareth them. We are of God: he that knoweth God heareth us; he that is not of God heareth not us. Hereby know we the spirit of truth and the spirit of error." 1 John 4:6.

Those who have been regenerated, more especially those who have received the Holy Spirit in sanctifying power, are able to detect false teaching. As John says, they "know the spirit of truth and the spirit of error;" the divine illumination of the Spirit in them enables them to guard against the modernistic false teachers who would take away from Christ His Deity and the atoning merit of His death; but the multitudes who have been received into the churches without regenerating grace, who have no spiritual illumination, are easily deceived and led away, not only by modernistic teachers, but the various cults that are so prevalent in the world today; hence, the tremendous importance of the ministry being careful to insist on regeneration of the individual prior to being received into the church.

In the sixth chapter of the Epistle to the Ephesians we find a statement that should fasten itself upon the mind of every child of God. After urging us to go on unto perfection, the Apostle says, "For it is impossible for those who were once enlightened, and have tasted of the heavenly gift, and were made partakers of the Holy Ghost, and have tasted of the good word of God, and the powers of the world to come, if they shall fall away, to renew them again unto repentance; seeing they crucify to themselves the Son of God afresh, and put him to an open shame."

We see here that there is such a thing as a falling away which seals the doom of that unfortunate soul who passes over the boundary line where repentance and pardon become impossible. It is evident that the Apostle is not speaking of backsliding, which, unfortunately, is quite common. You will find many who will admit that, since their regeneration, they have drifted away from their Lord, lost their peace and assurance of pardon, and that they are living in sin. The Scriptures offer such pardon and restoration, and in our revival meetings it is very common to see people of this character restored to the Lord and happy again in their fellowship with Him.

The Apostle gives here, a very clear statement of conditions that accompany the New Birth. It is quite interesting and remarkably descriptive. They have "tasted the heavenly gift" of forgiveness. They feel and know they have received pardon, a most blessed experience, and were "made partakers of the Holy Ghost." The Holy Ghost witnesses to every regenerated soul. How warm, peaceful and happy the heart into which the Spirit brings the sense of sins forgiven, and of a new life imparted. The Apostle also says, "have tasted the good word of God, and the powers of the world to come." The saving faith in Christ, of the penitent, brings all this. The word of God has a new and gracious meaning, and doubtless, there is a foretaste of heaven itself; peace with God, through our Lord and Saviour Jesus Christ, and the joy, a new and unearthly joy, comes to the regenerated soul. It is a bit of heaven on earth; heaven within the newborn child of God; doubtless a foretaste of that which remains in its fulness for those who are faithful unto the end.

Now, what does the Apostle mean about the falling away to a place where there is no repentance, and can be no pardon? No doubt it is the great sin of the re-crucifixion of Christ. It is the sin of those modernists who deny his Godhead, who sweep away from them and their deceived hearers all of prophecy concerning Jesus; all that Jesus claimed for Himself with reference to His oneness with the Father, of His pre-existence, of His atonement made upon the cross for sin; men who were once enlightened by pardoning mercy, and have known the gracious experience that comes to those who trust in Christ for forgiveness, and who were led away by deceivers, and repudiated Christ, with all He means to believers. They have "recrucified the Son of God." Have you noticed how cheerful they are in their skepticism and false teaching? How haughty and insolent their attitude of superiority and their contempt for the faithful? How rarely, if ever, you hear of repentance or restoration of such men.

We agree with the Apostle that, it is impossible for them to be restored to the divine favor, and to personal salvation. Such a state is impossible to any one who rejects Jesus Christ as the Son of God, the crucified, risen and glorified Saviour of men. They have no Christ for themselves, or to offer to any one else. It is a startling fact, but no doubt true, that they have fallen away and their salvation is impossible. Of course, any one who repents, who confesses and repudiates his or her unbelief, and comes back to the Christ of the Holy Scriptures may receive pardon; but the trouble with this arrogant group is, they do not repent; they are stubborn, conceited and fixed in their unbelief, and become more aggressive in their attacks upon Jesus and every phase of evangelical faith, revivals, holiness of heart, and the baptism with the Holy Spirit.

We say without hesitation, there are no Christians who have peace with God and assurance of the forgiveness of sins, and the witness of the Spirit to everlasting life, who reject the Virgin Birth, and therefore, the Godhead of Christ and the merits of the atonement He made upon the cross. God has shut up salvation in Jesus. "No man knoweth the Father save the Son, and he to whom the Son will reveal him." Woe and an eternity of darkness await all those men, however brilliant, educated and popular, who have joined with the ancient Jews in rejecting the Godhead of Jesus, have recrucified the Son of God by their false teaching, have led multitudes astray and are without God and, in the nature of things, must be without any witness of the Holy Spirit of their acceptance with God. And so, from a brother's heart, I warn and entreat the children of God to give no ear to any teacher who denies the Virgin Birth, the miracles wrought by our Lord, His claims to His oneness with the Father, and the atonement which He made for our sins upon the cross.

PRAYER.

Our Father in heaven, we humbly pray that the Holy Spirit may graciously guide all who read these words so that, they may not only believe that Jesus Christ is thy Son, but that they may so trust in Him that they may receive forgiveness of sin, and so walk with Him in the light, that they may understand their need of purity of heart and righteousness of life, and trust Him for that gracious cleansing received by the baptism with the Holy Spirit, and that, exercising this faith, they may be kept and finally presented to thee without spot or wrinkle, in that great day. We ask this, with all things, in the name of thy Son, our Lord and Saviour Jesus Christ. Amen!

THE CHASTENINGS OF THE LORD.

"Furthermore we have had fathers of our flesh which corrected us, and we gave them reverence: shall we not much rather be in subjection unto the Father of spirits, and live? For they verily for a few days chastened us after their own pleasure; but he for our profit, that we might be partakers of his holiness."
—Heb. 12:9, 10.

Sin, suffering and sorrow are triplets. Sin was born first; suffering and sorrow immediately followed, and they are as universal as the human race. The problem of suffering is one of the most difficult of solution that confronts us; it knocks at every door, is insistent and enters every human habitation, from the palace of the king to the hut of the beggar.

There are no conditions in life, no state of grace, no depth of humility, height of faith, or promise in Holy Writ that secure us against suffering and sorrow. There is assurance of consolation and comfort in any and every condition and circumstance that may befall us. There is a promise that the Divine Hand will make our bed in our sickness.

The consolations of the Word of God are at the call and command of all true followers of Christ. It is an interesting fact that many of the most consecrated and devout followers of Jesus have endured great physical suffering, and have had to pass through heartbreaking sorrow. One of the most serious features about sin is that its evil effects can be entailed; innocent children may have to suffer for the wickedness, immorality and intemperate lives of their ancestors, to the third and fourth generation. This gives us some conception of the fearful effect of the violations of divine law that should rule in our entire being.

Much of disease and sickness can be traced directly to intemperance of some sort. "Whatsoever a man soweth, that shall he also reap," covers a vast field of human activity. It appears from the text that God sends chastisements upon His children. Devout, courageous and faithful as Paul was, he had his thorn in the flesh. There was a purpose in it: "Lest he be exalted above measure." Paul tells us he prayed three times for the removal of the thorn, but God refused to remove the difficulty, which no doubt, was some physical suffering, but gave added grace. This is encouraging.

The case of Job gives us an interesting subject for thoughtful consideration. We find that, although, God pronounced him perfect, He permitted Satan to make frequent and severe attacks upon him. Robbers carried away his wealth; his children were killed in a windstorm; his bodily afflictions were so severe and offensive that his wife wished him dead. His best friends accused him of hypocrisy, but in it all, and through it all, he could, and did say of God, "I will trust in him, though he slay me." Early in the history of the race God determined through Job to reveal to Satan and mankind that a man, by obedience and faith, can unite himself to his Maker and Redeemer so that no power can break him asunder, but bereft of all material things, tortured with disease, and forsaken by all human help, he can shout in the face of death, "I know that my Redeemer liveth," and I shall live again.

Jesus once healed a blind man and the disciples asked Him this stupid question, "Who did sin? This man or his parents, that he was born blind?" "Jesus answered, Neither hath this man, nor his parents sinned," causing his blindness, but that "the glory of God might be revealed in him." Here we have a sunburst of light on the subject of human suffering and disappointment. The parents had sorrowed over their blind babe, had seen him grow to manhood, with deep regret. The man had suffered inconvenience, and perhaps, poverty, because of his blindness. No doubt the neighbors had shaken their dull, ignorant heads and said, seriously, "Your sins will find you out. We have been looking for some calamity to befall that couple. They have been holding their heads too high." Who of us has not judged, and often misjudged, our neighbors who had suffered some loss or affliction? It turns out, however, that there was a divine purpose in it all. God was going to glorify Himself by opening this man's eyes, and he was to become a devoted witness for Christ. How happy the man and his parents must have been!

The text gives us a multiplication table with which to figure out some of the perplexing mysteries of life. Take the context: "Whom the Lord loveth, he chasteneth, and scourgeth every son whom he receiveth." Well, that's comforting! In all well regulated families from which come the men and women who are the moral and spiritual salt of the community and church, there is discipline; the rod, not of cruelty and hatred, but of wisdom and love.

I desire us to get well fixed in our minds the objectives in the mind of our heavenly Father when He lays the chastening rod upon us. Let me read the text again: "But he for our profit that we might be partakers of his holiness." The final end in view, we stand appalled; for the moment we are speechless. Think of it! God is striving to bring us into such a state of submission to His divine will that He may fashion us, make us within our very being, like Himself, free from sin. My Lord, and my God! it is wonderful to contemplate! Thou art striving to bring us to open up all the doors of our being, that thou mayest enter into us, that we may become temples fit for thine indwelling; partakers of thy holiness; not something apart from thyself, but thine own eternal righteousness imparted to us; not to fix us so we cannot be tempted or cannot sin, but so, when we are tempted, there is within us no response to the tempter; the carnal nature is eradicated; thy holiness has come into us.

Peter has spoken to us of the exceeding great and precious promises by which we become partakers of the di-

THE PRESENCE OF GOD 27

vine nature. Now we see that the bed of our sufferings may become the cross upon which our old man is crucified, from which we may arise with the body of sin destroyed, and henceforth, being made free from sin, may yield the fruits of holiness, and in the end, have everlasting life. Then thanks be to God, for the chastening rod which brings into us the humility, the surrender, the consecration and the faith that enable us to partake of the holiness of God Himself.

Notice, my friendly reader, the sufferings of the body do not, and cannot, atone for the sins of the soul. The blood of Christ shed on Calvary is the only sin-cleansing power in the universe. We must come to that fountain for cleansing. "What can wash away my sin? Nothing but the blood of Jesus. What can make we whole again? Nothing but the blood of Jesus. O, precious is the flow, that makes me white as snow; no other fount I know; nothing but the blood of Jesus."

The chastenings of the Lord humble

us; reveal to us our weakness, our dependence and bring us to Christ as our only hope. It was when the prodigal son had wasted all of his substance in riotous living, and found he was perishing with hunger, that he determined to go back to his father's house, willing to be a servant. This very willingness to be a servant made it possible for him to be received as a son, with robe, and ring, and shoes, and a feast of joy and gladness.

In my boyhood I knew a handsome and successful young man. He prospered, married a woman of means; he became wealthy, proud and worldly; his health failed; men associated with him in business took advantage of his absence in a sanitarium and robbed him of his wealth, and eventually, destroyed his business. When he came home, weak and worn, he found himself in financial ruin; soon afterward he came to me full of joy and praise and said, "Henry, I was prosperous. My business succeeded; money flowed into me; I drifted away from God, I lost Christ out of my life, but the Lord has chastened me. I have lost my wealth, but I have found the Lord Jesus. My soul is happy. I thank God He has chastened me into the arms of His mercy and the compassion of His love."

When Brother J. L. Piercy and I made our evangelistic tour of the world we held a gracious revival in Port Said, Egypt. In that meeting a very prominent Englishman and his wife were converted at the altar of prayer. They invited us to tea in their home and said to us, "We have been worldly, wicked people. When free from the business cares of life we danced, played cards, and went to shows and gave no thought to God and souls. We had a beautiful little daughter, a wonderfully attractive child, who was taken ill and, in spite of every effort, died. It broke our hearts. We were in desolation; we did not know which way to turn; the world lost its charm for us, but we knew nothing of the consolations of religion. Some one invited us to your meetings, and thank God, we are saved, our dark problem is solved. We were unfit, utterly so, to raise our darling and God took her to Himself and brought us to repentance and saving faith in Christ." Multitudes in heaven and on their way thither, could give like testimony.

Reader, art thou chastened of the Lord? Has your property been swept away? Is your health gone? Has some loved one been caught away from you? Be sure that you are exercised by these chastenings of the Lord. Come to Him. Thank Him for His chastening mercies and open wide your being to receive His divine nature, cleansing, filling and keeping you until that glad day when we shall crown Jesus King of kings and Lord of lords.

PRAYER.

Our Father in Heaven, grant that the Holy Spirit may so reveal Jesus Christ in His fulness to all who may read this message, that there shall be no doubt of His Godhead and His power to forgive all transgressions, to cleanse from all sin, and to keep unspotted from the world. Grant us an answer to this prayer, in all who may read this message. For Christ's sake. Amen.

THE PRESENCE OF GOD.

"Whither shall I go from thy spirit? or whither shall I flee from thy presence? If I ascend up into heaven, thou art there; if I make my bed in hell, behold, thou art there. If I take the wings of the morning, and dwell in the uttermost parts of the sea: even there shall thy hand lead me, and thy right hand shall hold me."—Psalm 139:7-10.

King David, poet, prophet and song writer of Israel, is contemplating the omnipresence of God, which he describes in most eloquent and impressive language. The presence of God everywhere, and always, is a fact upon which we will do well to meditate.

A devout priest once said, "A memory of the presence of God is the best preventive against sin. Choose that place to sin where God is not." A wise exhortation, which leaves no time or place for sin. The presence of those persons for whose intelligence and excellence of character we have a high regard has a restraining and elevating effect upon us. We are greatly influenced for good or evil by the company we keep. The thought that God is everywhere, that His eye is upon us, that His ears hear every word we utter, that no thought or imagination is hidden from Him, ought to deliver us out of temptation, lift us high above the realm of wilful sin, and create within us an intense "hungering and thirsting after righteousness."

Forgetfulness of God, His presence, His laws for our guidance and protection, is sure to lead to sin of every kind. If men would keep two of the Commandments of Holy Writ, they could never forget the divine presence. One is the strict observance of the Sabbath, the other is the careful paying of the tithe. To keep the Sabbath with devout reverence, and to pay the tithe with careful honesty is to make forgetfulness of God impossible; if added to this are daily seasons of prayer, one is not likely to forget God or to wander away from Him. It would make the keeping of all the Commandments a part of a

THE PRESENCE OF GOD

peaceful and useful life.

Rev. Charles Finney was one of the greatest and most fruitful evangelists this country has produced. He would go into a city or community and preach to the people about God, His presence, His holiness, the justice of His laws, His right to rule among men, the graciousness of His mercy, the severity of His judgments upon those who refused the offers of His salvation. He would present, and urged these great Bible truths upon the people until they would become conscious of the divine presence. They would feel that God was in their midst. Their sins would become exceeding sinful, and they would cry out for mercy. Great revivals of religion would break out, deepen, spread and abide.

The times in which we are living call for such a ministry and such a message. Multitudes of our people, both within and outside of any church, have forgotten God; they neither think of, reverence nor love Him. His laws are violated with utter indifference; His mercies are neglected with no thought of the fearful consequences. The theory of creation by a process of evolution has banished God out of the thought of millions of our people, and put him so far away, and so indifferent to us and our problems, with a host of others, that God means nothing to them.

The results of this state of things are seen on every hand. Family religion is on the wane, marriage vows are no longer sacred with multitudes of our people. Youth, undisciplined, has become criminal, and in thousands of instances blasphemous. Many great seats of learning have become centers of atheism, and the breeding of all sorts of views and teachings, not only antagonistic to the Church, but to our constitution and democratic form of government; worst of all, there has crept into thousands of the pulpits of the nation a modernistic skepticism which questions and contradicts practically every fundamental doctrine of evangelical Christianity. "The wicked, through the pride of his countenance, will not seek after God: God is not in all his thoughts." Psalm 10:4.

The country is flooded with a literature that is intellectual and spiritual poison. The entertainments of the people are vulgar and indecent; brutal prizefights draw the cheering multitudes, Sabbath desecration is all about us. Distillers of intoxicants enlarge their plants, and millions of our people are becoming drunkards, both young and old, male and female. What shall the attitude and the answer of the faithful be? Shall it be indifference, or discouraged and saddened silence? God forbid.

"Where is the Lord God of Elijah." He still exists. He is in the midst of us. If we cleanse our ways, hands and hearts, and place our all upon the altar of consecration He will answer by fire in a way to confuse and confound the enemies of truth and righteousness.

The times and conditions in which we are living call for a ministry filled with the Holy Spirit, and a message that will bring upon the people a consciousness of the presence of God, His mercies to the penitent, and His fearful judgments upon those who violate His laws and reject His mercies. The people must be awakened to the fact that God is here in the midst of us, and that His mercies must be sought, His name reverenced, His laws obeyed, or wreckage and ruin of all that is good and beautiful in our nation are certain.

Our assault must be made upon Heaven, upon our knees; it must be persistent, a cry of distress in the all-prevailing name of Jesus Christ. We must have another pentecost of cleansing and empowering, like the crashing thunder of God in the days when faithful Samuel discomfited the Philistines. We must have displays of God's power among men that will sweep away the combined powers of wickedness, or chaos awaits us, and awaits but a short while.

Friendly reader, we are immortal beings in a boundless universe, with eternity stretching out before us. We can never get away from God. If we ascend into heaven His glory there will be our eternal joy; if we descend into hell His presence there will be our torment. If we are true to Him here, and the winds of adversity drive us into the uttermost parts of the seas, His hands of mercy and power will guide and hold us there.

PRAYER.

Our Father in heaven, give us such a sense of thy presence that we shall be kept from sin against thee. May thy Holy Spirit fill and guide us always in harmony with thy word and will, we humbly ask in the name of our Lord Jesus Christ. Amen.

FORGIVENESS.

If ye forgive not men their trespasses, neither will your Father in heaven forgive your trespasses. Matt. 6:15.

In His Sermon on the Mount Jesus gave to His disciples, for themselves, and for all His disciples in all the world to the end of time, a form of prayer. In this prayer He taught us to pray for forgiveness, as we forgive. The prayer finished, He comments on only one item, that of forgiveness, assuring us we shall be forgiven even as we forgive; also declaring if we forgive not men their trespasses neither will your Father in heaven forgive your trespasses. This statement is of divine authority, positive, clear and final.

In all of His teaching Jesus is careful to show us that we cannot be right with God and wrong with our fellowmen. He says, "Render therefore unto Cæsar the things that are Cæsar's; and unto God the things that are God's." This statement of Christ is illuminating, far-reaching and covers the whole territory of transaction between men and all their various relationships. It stands looking over a man's shoulder when he makes out his income tax report; it listens to him when he fixes the value upon his possessions to the legal assessor. It is a nice thing to be careful and exactly honest in everything, all of the time, in our dealings with our fellowmen. The whole tenor of the teaching of Christ is to the effect that if we wish to have peace with God we must not only be honest with our fellowmen but we must also be forgiving and merciful.

There is another teaching of Jesus that is quite searching, which reads like this: "If thou bring thy gift to the altar, and there rememberest that thy brother hath ought against thee; leave there thy gift before the altar, and go thy way: first be reconciled to thy brother, and then come and offer thy gift." Matt. 5:23, 24.

Rather exacting you say, and sometimes inconvenient, causing delay with the offering. Very well, there is the clear teaching of our Lord. If we expect God to accept our gift, hear our prayers, forgive our sins, or bless our souls, we must live in harmony with the teachings of His Son. Jesus goes even further than this, when He says, "But whosoever shall smite thee on thy right cheek, turn to him the other also. And if a man will sue thee at the law and take away thy coat, let him have thy cloak also. And whosoever shall compel thee to go a mile, go with him twain." These sayings of our Lord are taken from the Sermon on the Mount. This lifts up a standard for the true disciple of Christ, which is non-resisting in a high degree. I grant you that this sort of living is impossible to the natural man; man in his own strength will fail, but with Christ he can measure up to these standards. Christ in us the hope of glory makes all things possible.

This is a sinful world in which we are living. Man is a fallen, selfish, sinful being, and we may expect dishonest dealings, mistreatment, sometimes in the most unreasonable and provoking manner. The old carnal nature, even in a regenerated man under provocation, may give slap for slap and seek revenge if his coat is dishonestly taken away from him. But if the Old Man is crucified, the body of sin destroyed, and the root of bitterness uprooted and the Holy Spirit indwells us, we shall be equal to all the teachings and requirements of our Lord. "My grace is sufficient for thee." A commandment of God is equal to a promise; He is ready to supply the grace and power which will enable us to live up to all He requires.

What is the compensation if we live and act in harmony with the teachings of Jesus? There is a present peace, love, joy, and victory over any temptation that may come, and any difficulties that may arise. And those who live carefully in harmony with the teachings of Jesus may claim that wonderful promise which He gives us in John 14:21: "He that hath my commandments, and keepeth them, he it is that loveth me: and he that loveth me shall be loved of my Father, and I will love him, and will manifest myself to him." Again in the same chapter, 23rd verse, we have this wonderful promise of our Lord. It was in answer to an inquiry by Judas, not Iscariot, "Lord, how is it that thou wilt manifest thyself unto us, and not unto the world?" The answer of Christ was as follows: "Jesus answered and said unto him, if a man love me, he will keep my words: and my Father will love him, and we will come unto him, and make our abode with him." That is a marvelous promise of good company, and it is abiding. It is not a visitation occasionally, but the promise is "will make our abode with him." This is one of the most remarkable assurances of a gracious Christian experience, a blessed consciousness of the abiding presence of both the Father and the Son, which no doubt will enable us to resist all temptation, and to live in accordance with the highest standard we find in the teachings of our Lord for the guidance of our lives,

THE PRESENCE OF GOD 43

whatever condition may arise, or provoking trials may come to test us.

In a ministry of more than half a century I have met with many people who have gone through most of their lives with a grudge in their heart against some one whom they felt had done them wrong. Perhaps a member of their own family, a brother or sister in the church of which they were members; they attended the services, supported the church with their money and, to all outward appearance, were living consistently, but had hatred and unforgiveness in their heart, and no peace or joy in their religious life. Their religious experience is not only blighted but their religious influence is destroyed; they stand in the way of revivals, and hinder the work of God.

Some years ago I was engaged for a revival in a Methodist Church in one of the county seats of Kentucky. Some one who was acquainted with conditions in that church said, "You cannot have a revival. There has not been one there in twenty years. That church is divided by hard feeling and an unforgiving spirit in two of the leading families of the congregation, and has been crippled in its religious life and activities for twenty years."

It would be hard to estimate the harm that had been done by these unforgiving people, the good work that had been hindered, the souls that had been lost; but for this spirit of unforgiveness there might have been revivals during the many years, hundreds of souls converted and sanctified; devout young men would possibly have entered the ministry, and missionaries gone to foreign fields; but these poor, stubborn, unforgiving hearts had grieved the Holy Spirit, had practically tied the hands of a number of pastors. They were prominent families, and in their conceit and hardness of heart they had no conception of the hurt they had wrought and the harm they had done.

We had a gracious revival in the church, and some of the old animosities were swept away. Some of these mem-

THE PRESENCE OF GOD 45

bers who had hated each other had died, the Lord had removed them in their sins, and the Lord gave us a gracious victory. The church entered upon a new life; many of the old members rejoiced that the things which had hurt and hindered for so long had finally disappeared through death and removal to other places, rather than forgiveness and reconciliation.

Sometime ago I was in a community that had its family troubles. A wealthy farmer with a large family of children had died leaving considerable estate. The children were dissatisfied with the will and there arose strife and hatred among them. The lawyers were getting quite a good share of the estate. A gentleman in the community told me that one of the lawyers who represented one of the sons of the old man said that this client of his had come into his office and talked very sadly of the trouble and division that had arisen in the family that had lived so happily together up to the death of his father. The farmer said, "It is very distressing; all harmony and peace have broken up among us. Brother John will not speak to Brother Will's wife, John's wife is so mad at my wife she will not speak to her; the children of the family have gotten the spirit of division and hatred, and sometimes when I think about the trouble we are having over the estate, the division and strife among us, I almost wish father had not died."

This was by no means an isolated case. I think I could write a rather interesting book on instances that have occurred in revival meetings revealing hatred and a spirit of unforgiveness among prominent church members, who were active so far as attending church was concerned, and paying their money, but with a spirit of hatred within their hearts. Evidently the Holy Spirit cannot dwell in a heart in which hatred abides.

The statements of our Lord in the text are very clear and from them there is no appeal. We must forgive. I remember well in my early ministry I became angry with a man; there is no

THE PRESENCE OF GOD

doubt he was a bad man. The last I heard of him he was in jail in a southern city for leaving his own wife and running away with another man's wife. I found that when I permitted anger to arise in my heart against the bad man that all peace went out. I preached four times, two Sabbaths morning and evening, without any peace, unction or joy. I was miserable. The dove had departed; the raven sat upon the door saying "never more." I fasted and prayed, but no answer. I went deep into the woods. I gathered up brush, made a brush pile, lay on top of it face down and wept and cried to God to forgive my hatred and give me grace to love a wicked man, that I believed to be guilty of great wrong. Do you ask why I made the brush pile and did not lie upon the ground? It had rained, the ground was damp and cold, I was afraid that if I should lie upon the ground I would catch cold and it might go into pneumonia and I might die, and I felt sure I was in no condition to enter heaven.

This distress of mine lasted for something over two weeks, but I prayed through to complete victory and I could say in my heart, "Father, forgive him, he knows not what he does. He is in darkness and ignorance of the ways of righteousness." I felt I could gladly and happily embrace him. The raven at once departed and the dove of peace came back, and what sweet and restful peace it was. I learned that, however devout and earnest you may be, it does not grant you the privilege to hate the most wicked man, but if you would have forgiveness and the peace and joy which forgiveness brings we must forgive.

And now, O reader, how is it with thy soul? Is there any hatred there, any unforgiveness, any spirit of resentment? Watch and pray against the encroachment of any such thing into thy mind. Keep close to Jesus, keep the spirit of His love and mercy and forgiveness, and no doubt peace and joy will permanently abide with you.

PRAYER.

Our Heavenly Father, grant, we beseech thee, that every one who reads this message may have within their hearts the witness that he or she has been born again, and have that peace of mind that passeth all understanding. Help us to remember that, if we expect forgiveness from thee we shall have to forgive those who have wronged us, for thou hast told us, "If ye forgive not men their trespasses, neither will your Father in heaven forgive your trespasses." We ask this in the name of our Lord and Saviour Jesus Christ. Amen.

THE NEW BIRTH.

"Marvel not that I said unto thee, Ye must be born again." John 3:7.

The coming of Nicodemus to Christ by night does not suggest to me that he was a cowardly man, and for that reason did not come more openly in the day time. Nicodemus was an intelligent, sincere, devout man; he believed Jesus to be a teacher sent from God. He came to Christ quietly in the night, not for disputation or controversy, but to know the truth about who Jesus was, and His mission in the world. It was because of this state of mind that Jesus at once gave him the very heart and center of the gospel. "Except a man be born again, he cannot see the kingdom of God."

Nicodemus thought Jesus was speaking of a new physical birth and marveled, saying, "How can a man be born when he is old?" Jesus explained that he was not speaking of a physical, but of a spiritual birth, reiterating His assertion not only to Nicodemus but to all men for all time, "Marvel not that I

THE PRESENCE OF GOD

said unto thee, ye must be born again."

In his teaching our Lord often used parables, figures, and striking contrasts in order to make the great truths of divine revelation easy of comprehension. He could not have chosen a better figure than that of birth to illustrate the gracious work of the Holy Spirit in the individual by which such individual is recreated, born again, regenerated, made in Christ a new creature.

Our Lord Jesus was never more emphatic in any of His teachings than in this strong statement, "Ye must be born again" in order to enter into the Kingdom of God. There must be a change so radical, so gracious, and so wonderful in one's nature in order to become a child of God that Jesus calls it a birth, the coming into a man of a new conscious life, a translation from the kingdom of Satan, darkness and death, into the kingdom of God, light and life. With this plain teaching of Jesus on this important subject, and the experience of multiplied thousands who are faithful witnesses to the regenerating power of the Holy Spirit why should any one object to this new spiritual birth?

The teaching of Christ is very emphatic and positive with reference to this radical change in any individual before he or she can enter into the Kingdom of God. It must be remembered always that it is one thing to unite with some church organization and another, and a very different thing, to be born of the Spirit.

In order to the new birth there must be a consciousness of sin, a sense of being lost, and the need of a Saviour. The work of conviction is wrought by the Holy Spirit; He and He alone can reveal the turpitude of sin, the exceeding wickedness of the violation of divine law. He can give to the sinner's intelligence a sense of feeling of his guilt that cannot possibly be wrought in him by any sort of human argument or influence. Of course, the human may be instrumental, but the Holy Spirit is the divine agent that uncovers the sinful life and awakens the conscience and illuminates the mind, and brings to the individual a profound sense of being a sinner, lost, and in need of a Saviour. This work of conviction for sin wrought by the Holy Spirit is a very important foundation work in the beginning of the building of Christian character. No one can understand the need of salvation and approach Christ in the proper spirit of faith for the supply of that need until they have had a profound sense of their own sinfulness and guilt before God.

Sometime ago, just after I pronounced the benediction, while holding a series of revival meetings, a young man with an intelligent face, with sort of a sneer, walked up to me and said, "Do you mean to say that the pulling of a little thing like an apple started all of this sin and sorrow and ruin we see in the world?" "O," I said, "it might have been a gooseberry. The pulling of the apple was the violation of a divine command, and to wilfully violate a divine command of God is not a little thing, and may lead on to most tremendous, widespread, and disastrous results." His face changed in its expression, he dropped his head and looked at the floor for a moment, turned around and walked away. Some person ignorant of the operations of the Spirit upon the human mind in bringing a soul through the processes that are consummated in the New Birth said, "Why should little children weep at an altar of prayer? They have never been great sinners; there certainly is no need for great sorrow or repentance upon their part." The simple truth is they are under conviction, the Holy Spirit has revealed to them the fact that they are lost. The simplest act of disobedience appears to them in its real light and they are conscious of the fact that there are no little sins; that, having sinned, they are lost; they cry out for mercy, and quite properly so, and if correctly taught it will not be difficult to assist them to exercise saving faith in Christ; and throughout a long life and all eternity they will remember that they were once lost sinners, and were without hope or help,

THE PRESENCE OF GOD

apart from the compassion and saving power of the Lord Jesus.

How unfortunate that ministers who do not want to go through the travail of soul in prayer that brings a revival should substitute a *decision day* and bring into the church great droves of children who have never known anything of conviction for sins wrought by the Holy Spirit, a sense of their lostness and their need of a Saviour. Fill up the church with persons who have substituted a human decision for the mighty works of the Holy Spirit in conviction and regeneration and you have a people who have not and cannot have any sort of spiritual insight, or intelligent understanding of what the New Birth means; of what it is to be a lost sinner saved by grace.

Such persons coming into the church without conviction, without repentance, without the New Birth, without the witness of the Holy Spirit, without any of the consolations or joys of salvation, and are still under the dominion of their carnal nature, are still of the world and love the things of the world. Bring into the church worldly amusements, plays, pastimes, and the things that appeal to the unregenerated, and your church becomes paralyzed, so far as any sort of spiritual evangelism and soul winning are concerned. Such persons become the easy victims of false teaching, as they have no spiritual anchorage or illumination. They are still dead in trespasses and in sins. When they read the scriptures with reference to the joy and peace that are pledged to the faithful followers of Christ, they have no such peace or joy or gracious witness of the Spirit that they are saved; naturally, questions will arise in their mind as to whether or not these scriptures are divinely inspired. They become the easy victims of modernistic teaching, or they can be led away by many of the unscriptural and dangerous cults that are in the world, ready to lead captive these souls that have never been born of the Spirit, and who are in darkness and uncertainty, sometimes trying to work out their salvation by sheer human methods, rather than in harmony with the teachings of our Lord.

Nothing ever happened in Methodism more unfortunate than the plan for a *decision day* in which bright and intelligent children are catechized, received into the church, without any illumination, conviction, or operation of the Holy Spirit. They will grow up in a state of uncertainty of mind about everything sacred. Spiritual things must be spiritually discerned, and they have no such discernment, and so it comes to pass many churches are filled up very largely with an unregenerated, dancing, card-playing, movie-going multitude, who are utterly worldly. The sinful world about them knows such church members to be like themselves, has no faith in their professions, and comes to look upon the church as a great farce, so far as its living the Christ life is concerned.

You cannot save a lost world with a worldly church. The result is that we have great numbers of churches, especially in our cities, that never undertake a revival of religion. They would not understand a spiritual ministry that would produce conviction and bring sinners to repentance. I heard a devout woman not long since who was a member of a prominent Methodist church say, "I have been a member of that church for fifteen years, quite regular in my attendance, have paid into it many hundreds of dollars, and in these fifteen years I have seen two young people kneel at the altars of the church for a few moments who got up without any appearance of a change of heart, were received into the church and were sent away apparently with the impression that they had become Christians." What a travesty! I can but believe that ministers who trifle in this way with the souls of the people will have to face some fearful facts in the day of judgment.

There is complaint among thoughtful people everywhere that there is a great spiritual slump in the church, and in the general morals of society, that there

THE PRESENCE OF GOD

is a heavy current drifting away from everything that is sacred and of real spiritual value among men. No doubt this is true, and it *is* true because many ministers have ceased to insist upon the New Birth, true repentance and a faith in Christ which brings the witness of the Spirit that sins have been forgiven and a sweet and blessed assurance that one has found in Jesus a personal conscious Saviour.

We grant that the regenerating work of the Holy Spirit is mysterious. We do not understand, nor do we need to understand, how that, in a moment a sinner can be saved, a lost and wretched penitent can become a rejoicing child of God, a new creature in Christ. This divine work is a mystery profound, deep and high. But we can have the assurance within our own consciousness that the work has been done.

In this conversation with Nicodemus our Lord reveals the fact that the human part of the transaction is faith in Christ. As the serpent was lifted up in the wilderness and those who were bitten and dying looked and lived, so whatever our sins, however many, deep and dark and awful, if we look to Christ with saving faith our sins are blotted out, and we receive an inward consciousness that we are born of the Spirit, and we can say "Abba Father"—"Our Father who art in heaven."

My friendly readers, have you been born again? Have you received the witness of the Holy Spirit that your sins have been forgiven? Can you say with a triumphant faith, "I know that my Redeemer liveth?" If so, may God help you to be faithful. If not, do not be content until you have a full assurance within your heart that Jesus is your Saviour, that your sins are blotted out, "And the Spirit witnesses to the blood that you have been born of God." This is your privilege. Let me urge you, as a brother, to be content with nothing less than a sweet and restful sense within your soul that Christ is your personal Saviour.

THE PRESENCE OF GOD

PRAYER.

Our Father in Heaven, we humbly and earnestly pray that some who read this message who have not been born of the Spirit may be profoundly convicted of sin, and led and taught through kindly human agencies, or by the Holy Ghost Himself, shall exercise genuine repentance, saving faith in Christ, and be born again. May they be led in the way of salvation, and finally into the heaven of eternal peace, into thy glorious presence. We ask for these mercies and blessings in the name of thy Son, our Lord and Saviour Jesus Christ. Amen.

THE FUTURE PUNISHMENT OF THE WICKED.

"Depart from me, ye cursed, into everlasting fire, prepared for the devil and his angels." Matt. 25:41.

In the teaching of our Lord from which we take the text, He gives us a startling view into the future; we have the assembled nations before Him as He sits upon His throne judging the people and separating the righteous from the wicked, as a shepherd, "divides his sheep from the goats."

The picture as presented to us by our Lord reveals the fact that His judgments will be severe on those who have refused the helping hand to those who are the least of His disciples. Has the reader noticed that, in Holy Writ, we have much of warning to the rich, and pleading for the poor? We could easily gather from the Old Testament and the New sufficient matter of this character to make a good sized booklet.

We readily understand that this teaching of our Lord in the 25th chapter of Matthew does not mean that Heaven and eternal life can be secured by charitable deeds, but it does mean that one must be so transformed by the renewing power of the Holy Spirit that he or she lives to serve. The religion of Jesus Christ is a religion of love, compassion, and glad helpfulness. When asked what was the first and great commandment the Lord did not stop with loving God supremely, but He added that we must love our neighbor as ourselves.

We note in the teaching of the text that the Lord says, "Depart from me, ye cursed, into everlasting fire, prepared for the devil and his angels." It appears from the reading of the text that when Satan rebelled against God many angels united with him in this rebellion and were cast out of Heaven. Saint Peter tells us that, "God spared not the angels that sinned, but cast them down to Hell, and delivered them into chains of darkness to be reserved unto judgment." 2 Peter 2:4.

It appears that this fearful prison

house for rebellious souls was not originally prepared for men, but for the devil and fallen angels; however, the Lord shows us that the selfish, wicked, and God-rejecting people shall finally be shut up in this fearful place of punishment and hopeless despair. We hear but little preaching upon the subject of future punishment; not a few preachers do not hesitate to flatly contradict the oft-repeated teachings of Christ on the subject of the punishment that awaits the impenitent wicked. Some prominent ministers do not hesitate to say that there is no such place as the Hell spoken of in the Scriptures, but that the people in the time of Christ believed there was such a place, and that Jesus knew no better than to believe the current ideas and beliefs of the people of His times.

When we consider the sinless character of the Christ, the wisdom of His sayings, the consistency of His teachings, the highness of His claims for Himself, the patience with which He suffered, the prayer He offered for those

THE PRESENCE OF GOD 65

who nailed Him to the cross, and ridiculed Him while He suffered there, His resurrection, and what His gospel has wrought among men in the world, we believe it is a serious and dangerous risk for any preacher to contradict His teachings on any subject; or to intimate that He was ignorant, and because of this, gave out warnings and teachings that are without any foundation in facts, for this or the future life.

Our Lord Jesus is not by any means the first teacher in Holy Writ claiming divine knowledge of the future, to speak of a Hell awaiting those who persistently trample upon divine law and reject divine mercy. David in the 9th Psalm, 16th and 17th verses says, "The Lord is known by the judgments which he executeth; the wicked is snared in the work of his own hands. The wicked shall be turned into Hell, and all the nations that forget God." Solomon, speaking of the folly of the man enticed from the path of virtue by the vile woman, says, "Her house is the way to Hell, going down to the chambers of death." And again, "But he knoweth not that the dead are there and that her guests are in the depths of Hell."

We understand that the modernistic, skeptical preacher will readily undertake to explain all this away, but he will hardly claim that the house of the fallen woman is an open door to Paradise. It must lead to some place. Many depart this life from the place of shameless sin who certainly are not in a state of purity to enter Heaven, or a state of mind to enjoy it. Death does not change one's nature, it simply changes his place of residence. He leaves this world and enters into a spirit world. If he was a sinner against God here, without repentance and saving faith in Christ, he is the same in that other world into which he is entering.

We read in Isaiah's address to fallen Lucifer as follows: "Hell from beneath is moved for thee to meet thee at thy coming; it stirreth up the dead for thee, even all the chief ones of the earth; it hath raised up from their thrones all

THE PRESENCE OF GOD 67

the kings of the nations. All they shall speak and say unto thee, Art thou also become weak as we? Art thou become like unto us? Thy pomp is brought down to the grave, and the noise of thy viols; the worm is spread under thee, and the worms cover thee. How art thou fallen from Heaven, O Lucifer, son of the morning! How art thou cut down to the ground, which didst weaken the nations!" Isa. 14:9-12. There is more of this address to fallen Lucifer from Isaiah, but the above is enough, and it shows where Satan himself will finally land, and also reveals the fact that those wicked and godless kings and rulers who lived in pomp and splendor, who have tyrannized over men, carried on wars of butchery and slaughter of the common people for their pastime, lived utterly selfish and godless, and left this world unrepentant in their sins, still are in a state of conscious existence, a "wormy" place of torment. We could hardly conceive of these monstors of selfishness and sin being assembled in a Paradise of peace and joy at the feet of Jesus. According to Isaiah they are not there, but in a place where there is no peace. They have gone beyond the reach of help or hope.

In the 5th chapter of Matthew we have from our Lord the following searching words: "And if thy right eye offend thee, pluck it out, and cast it from thee: for it is profitable for thee that one of thy members should perish, and not that thy whole body should be cast into hell. And if thy right hand offend thee, cut it off, and cast it from thee; for it is profitable for thee that one of thy members should perish, and not that thy whole body should be cast into hell." Matt. 5:29, 30.

In Luke 10th chapter and 15th verse, we have Jesus speaking to a crowd of impenitent, and wicked sinners: "And thou, Capernaum, which art exalted to heaven, shalt be thrust down to hell." Will those who contradict the teachings of Christ with reference to the future state of the wicked insist that Chicago, and New York cities, with all their wickedness, crime, corruption, graft, drunkenness, murders, shall be emptied into Paradise? Would heaven remain a place of purity and peace if these vast multitudes who have trampled upon all the laws of God, rejected all his offers of mercy, and challenged all his warnings of judgment, should indiscriminately be turned loose into the place where we understand can only be entered by the holy, by those whose spirits are in harmony with the Christ who has redeemed them, and with a sinless heaven of rest and peace and eternal joy.

In the 16th chapter of Luke Jesus gives us a most startling glimpse into the future. He seeks to so impress the truth contained in this parable or recitation of a historical event that He brings it before us in striking contrast. There is affluent wealth and extreme poverty; there is the contrast of robes and rags. One of the persons depicted is faring sumptuously every day, and the other is fortunate if, among the dogs, he gets a crumb or a bit of dirty meat out of the dust. A man in the palace arrayed in robes and feasting is selfish and sinful; the man in rags among dogs has beneath his lean and bony ribs purity of heart and faith in God. There comes a sudden change; the beggar dies and goes directly to Abraham's bosom, the haven of peace and rest. The rich man dies and lifts up his fruitless cry from hell, saying, "I am tormented in this flame," and begging for the moistened finger of Lazarus to cool his parched tongue.

Shall we insist that Jesus is trifling with humanity in this terrible picture of the future state of a selfish rich man and a humble beggar who has found robes and rest forever? Of course, we understand that Jesus is not teaching that all rich men will go into hell, and that all poor men will go into heaven; but Jesus is giving us faithful warning that at sundown a man might be living in a palace of splendor, robed in the finest fabrics, feasting among his courteous friends, and when the evening star comes out he may be crying in hell for help which can never come to him.

THE PRESENCE OF GOD 71

A great gulf fixed, over which no help can pass.

Jesus knows that our inclination is to desire riches and fear poverty, and in this bit of history He is teaching us that there is something far better than riches and far worse than poverty. He is not trifling with us but giving us a look into the future as a faithful warning that we may hasten to make our decisions and select the place in which we shall spend eternity. All the Scriptures teach us that God has no pleasure in death and destruction, but would that all men come to Christ; that the provisions of salvation are ample, that the gift of eternal life is free, that whosoever will may come, and that those who refuse to come, but continue in a state of rebellion, impenitence and sin will, in the nature of things, go out into darkness and torment.

There can be no order in this world or any other world without law. Law without penalty is dead and worthless. If penalty is not inflicted and the guilty punished we can have no civilization.

All progressive people have legislation for the arrest and punishment of thieves, murderers, incendiaries, and all criminals who disturb the peace and violate the laws for the just and equal organization of society. This must be so if we are to have anything worth the name of a progressive civilization, and a decent world to live in.

The same is true in God's moral universe. There are certain great laws that are as fixed and eternal as the character of God Himself. They are for the protection, the guidance, the uplift and salvation of society and of the individual. The Ten Commandments flow out of the same fountain of love and compassion from which comes the Sermon on the Mount. There are penalties attached to God's laws. In the nature of things this must be so; it is the inevitable logic of the universe. To the penitent, returning prodigal the arms of mercy are ever open; the white robe, the ring of holy covenant and the feast await the most wretched who come back in repentance; but for those

THE PRESENCE OF GOD 73

who will not come there is nothing left but outer darkness and eternal doom.

The question arises in the minds of many, Is the lake of fire of which Jesus speaks, literal? Is there actual burning fire, or is He using figures of speech? There is one thing of which we may be sure; if Jesus in speaking of the future punishment of the wicked is using figures of speech they do not exaggerate the facts. Jesus is incapable of exaggeration, and those who persist in rebellion against God in refusing to repent will eventually find that the place of their future abode, in the awfulness of its torment, is in perfect harmony with the teachings of Christ. And now, O reader, where will you spend eternity? If thou art a sinner, come to Christ for salvation. Never yet has He refused to hear the prayer of the penitent and answer the cry of a sinful soul for forgiveness. And if thou art a Christian hold fast to thy profession, be steadfast to the end, and do not fail to reach out a helping hand and win some lost soul to Christ.

PRAYER.

Our Father in Heaven, we humbly pray that the Holy Spirit may impress these solemn and awful truths upon those who may read this appeal of warning and entreaty; and may this message produce fruit in the salvation of immortal souls.

THE SEARCHINGS OF THE LORD.

"Search me, O God, and know my heart: try me, and know my thoughts: and see if there be any wicked way in me, and lead me in the way everlasting."—Psalm 139:23, 24.

Our text is a prayer and, no doubt, deeply sincere, of King David, offered while he was on the throne of Israel. We can hardly conceive of a man offering a prayer like this who has not a genuine and intense desire that his heart be pure and his life right before God.

David was a great man, deep and high and broad of soul. He was a great saint; and, sad to say, a great sinner. As a boy, I judge the greatest rock-thrower in Israel. Fortunate for David, the circumstances of his family were such that he had to work, and his job was that of shepherding his father's sheep. There were lions and bears in the community and they were mutton-hungry and David had to keep them away from the sheep under his protection; in those days they didn't have Winchester revolvers, not even old muzzle-loading muskets with flint-lock and powder-pans. He had to resort to rocks, and he could throw them with such accuracy and with such remarkable force that he actually killed a lion and a bear.

If David had been a son of luxury and idleness, or if the government had passed a law that the younger members of the family must do no work and live in idleness, he never would have developed the capacity for throwing rocks which enabled him with a stone to kill Goliath, the champion of the Philistine army, turn the enemies of his country to flight, and save his people from the ravages of an invading, pagan army. Blessed is the lad that doeth little things well in the early years of his life, for verily I say unto you, he will be able to do some large things that may count for the welfare of his nation when he has older grown.

I almost wish that I could forget David's sin. It was grievous, indeed, horrible. Can you think of anything worse than that a man should take the advantage of a brave soldier absent from his home, fighting the battles of his country, to debauch his wife? This is exactly what David did, and this is perhaps not the worst of it. This vile deed done, to hide his sin he arranged for the death of Uriah, the man whom he had so grievously wronged. He actually had this brave soldier, whom he could trust without fear with a confidential message, carry a note to Joab, the commander-in-chief of his army, with this remarkable paragraph in the message: "And he wrote in the letter, saying, Set Uriah in the forefront of the battle, and retire ye from him that he may be smitten, and die." Think of it! The brave man, who had been so deeply wronged, so trustworthy that he could risk him to carry his own death message in his hand, and think of Joab, whispering around among his soldiers and arranging to retire suddenly without Uriah knowing anything about it, to be smitten down, to cover the sin of a king lying around the palace, eating heartily, sleeping late, and cultivating his animal passions when he ought to have been at the front in his tent eating the plain fare of the camp and leading the hosts to victory. Indolence, much sleep, and the indulgence in rich food, is dangerous to any one. Such men are rare, if ever, pure in heart and righteous in life. Make a note of this and keep busy in the good work of the Lord, and in the service of your fellow beings.

I have always had a bit of suspicion about Uriah's wife. Husband is away at the battle and she has time to hatch up some schemes of her own. It is entirely possible that she secured a room near the palace and watched the habits of the king, and, knowing just about the time he would take a walk on the walls of the palace, she takes a bath and leaves up the window-blind. Note the sad results. But for this neglect of a small thing, you say, this dark and bloody chapter would never have been written in the life of David. Some one has said, "There are no little sins." Perhaps this saying is correct, but small things that are not plainly stamped with the insignia of sin may easily lead to sin of the deepest dye which may be forgiven but leave the scars and a certain stain in memory which cannot be washed out. What a pity Uriah's wife did not pull down the window-blind when she took her bath.

There is nothing more fatal to a man, however great and good he may be, than to permit himself to have a passionate desire for the wrong woman. It has been the downfall of multitudes. I could write a good-sized booklet on the sad history of men I have known, who were once strong and clean and endued with spiritual power, who turned to this fatal path, went down with a crash, lived in shame, and died in desolation.

It will not be improper to intimate that a designing, attractive woman is about as good fish-bait as Satan can put on his hook. She can plan and scheme, draw away from the path of rectitude and blast a body and soul, apparently without any sort of hesitation or consideration of breaking hearts, ruining homes, and blasting souls for this world and all other worlds.

I do not especially like this introduction to my sermon, but somehow it was in the top of my mind and I had to get it out in order to get to the deeper thought suggested by the text.

At the time David offers this prayer, he was no doubt in the state of mind described by the Lord Jesus when he said, "Blessed are they which do hunger and thirst after righteousness: for they shall be filled." Evidently the Psalmist was not willing to risk his own judgment with reference to himself. He is doubtless right in this. None of us should be willing to sit as a member of the jury that tries us. We are sure to be prejudiced in our own favor. No man can know himself apart from the teachings of the Lord, the illumination of the Holy Spirit, and so the Psalmist realizing that the time would come, which will come to us all, when we must be searched with the all-seeing eye in the great day of judgment, beseeches

God to search him.

That word, "search," is a good, strong word: leave nothing hidden; move all the furniture of my good thought, good intentions, and good deeds, anything of a deceitful character or perhaps some heavy chest or box shaded with hypocrisy. "Search me,"—move every obstacle out of the way; find any hidden thing; drag it out of its place of secrecy; leave nothing to damage me in my spiritual life here, or condemn me in that great day when I must appear in the white light of the final judgment. Listen to this man's prayer and let us lay hold upon it for our prayer: "Search me, O God, and know my heart." The heart is the center of our spiritual and moral being. Jesus tells us that it is the things that come out of the heart that defileth a man. An inspired writer says, "Out of the heart are the issues of life." The heart is the fountain from which flows the stream of thought, word, action, living, and if the heart be impure the stream must be impure. So we find this great man praying God to search his heart.

He goes a little further,—"know my thoughts." That is very important. We are not to forget that there is a thought-life. Thought kindles desire, desire leads to action, actions form habits, and habits, repeated, become a part of our very being, form character, make up what we are and, will continue to be, in all probability, not only while we live in the flesh, but while the immortal spirit lives after the flesh has gone back to the dust. How carefully we should guard the realm of our thoughts. The enemy understands this very vital feature in our soul-life and experience and will not fail to tempt us here. Vain imaginations may fill the mind; evil thoughts are the kindling wood that builds the fires of intense desire. So we should join David in asking God to help us in guarding and directing our thought-life. I must not overlook that expression, "Try me." David is asking God to try him; to put the test on him; see if I am what I ought to be in heart and thought. Listen as he goes for-

THE PRESENCE OF GOD

ward. "See if there is any wicked way in me, and lead me in the way everlasting."

This prayer makes it very clear that David desires a clean heart, pure thought, and a righteous life. And why not? Can we conceive of a Christian, one who has been born again and who is a child of God, being content with anything less than this? Can a child of God desire or be content with an impure heart? It would seem impossible to have such desire and remain a child of God. Not a few people who claim to be Christians sneer at the idea of sanctification and manifest no sort of desire to be holy. Is this sort of thing consistent? What is sanctification? It is an operation of the Holy Spirit cleansing away sin. That is the evangelical sense and meaning of this word which has attracted to itself so much controversy and reproach. Is it reasonable that a child of God should be content with anything less than a pure heart, a heart, as Charles Wesley sings, "From sin set free?" How would it sound for a member of the church, or a preacher in the pulpit to stand up and say, "I do not wish to be holy. I am quite content to have an impure heart, unclean and wicked thoughts, ambitious and un-Christlike desires?" I think that would startle us, and yet it would seem that a good many people would only speak the truth in harmony with their conduct and way of living if they should give a testimony of that character.

Undoubtedly, we are at a time in history when the church and religious life of this nation should have an awakening. We need a type of teaching in our religious literature, Sabbath school and otherwise, and a proclamation from our pulpits that will awaken in all church members of every faith and order a spirit of prayer like that expressed by the Psalmist in our text, a longing for the searchings of the Almighty, for the discovery of the eye of God, of everything contrary to the teachings of His Word, His love for us who are His children, and His desire that we

THE PRESENCE OF GOD 85

should be from sin set free; the practice of it, the power of it, the in-being of it; that we should be free from the inclination of any sort within or without to sin against God and humanity. Sin is not only against God, but it is against ourselves and our fellow-beings. It is a fearful thing in the breadth of its scope and influence, in the depth of its degradation and in the height of its conceit and pride from which, by and by, the perpetrator shall fall in fearful crash and ruin.

I kindly ask all readers of this message to join me in earnest prayer with a definite understanding that we make no reservation; that if the Lord finds something within us in our habits or business or plans that is contrary to His will, and therefore hurtful to us, we shall not only give Him leave to remove it, but we will join with the ancient poet of Israel and with genuine earnestness cry out, "Search me, O God, and know my heart: try me, and know my thoughts; and see if there be any wicked way in me, and lead me in the way everlasting." May we so breathe from our inmost souls the spirit of this prayer, repeat it, and insist upon it, that we shall be heard, and a compassionate God shall not only search us, try us, but find within us anything and everything that hinders our peace with Him and our service for Him and our fellowbeings, and remove it from us. No doubt He can do it. The blood of Jesus Christ, His Son, cleanseth us from all sin. Let us so commit ourselves, along with this prayer, that the answer be made possible that God may have His will in us and with us while life shall last, and then we shall find that, by faith we have been led in the way that has no end. It is everlasting. Amen.

THE BAPTISM WITH THE HOLY SPIRIT.

"If ye love me, keep my commandments. And I will pray the Father, and he shall give you another Comforter, that he may abide with you for ever; even the Spirit of truth; whom the world cannot receive, because it seeth him not, neither knoweth him: but ye know him; for he dwelleth with you, and shall be in you."—John 14:15, 16, 17.

In the thirty-third verse of the thirteenth chapter of John's Gospel, our Lord Jesus greatly saddened His disciples when He said, "Ye shall seek me: and as I said unto the Jews, whither I go, ye cannot come; so now I say to you."

The disciples had left their homes, their business, families, and everything to follow Jesus. They believed in Him and loved Him. Jesus was their religion. They did not fully comprehend Him, or the plan of His Kingdom, or the mission He had for them. Perhaps no one has ever been able with the finite mind to comprehend all of this. But the ecclesiastics were against them. At that time they had no organization. The church under the new dispensation had not been organized. They had no written creed or stated system of doctrine. *But they had Jesus.*

To follow Jesus, to look at Him, to love Him, to obey Him, was their religion; and now that He tells them that He is to be separated from them, they are in great distress. Jesus notes their state of mind and seeks to comfort them by saying, "Let not your hearts be troubled. Ye believe in God; believe also in me." The thought is, You do not see God, but you do not doubt His existence or question His fatherly care; and while you do not see me, you must believe me. He assured them that He would come again and receive them unto Himself.

With the organized church with its beautiful buildings of worship, its accumulation of institutions, its printed creeds and statements of doctrines, its many officials, overseers, leaders, and all of those things that naturally and properly accumulate with and in an organized church, it is not only quite probable, but we are in danger of getting so interested in the things of the Kingdom that we forget the King and go along with our many enterprises, institutions, and buildings, without Jesus in the midst, and perhaps, hardly in our thought. There is great necessity of careful guarding here.

Continuing His words of comfort, Jesus makes the very definite promise of the gift of the Holy Spirit as a Comforter to His followers; and we understand that this promise was not only to those disciples who were with Him, at the time, but it is for all of His disciples in all time to come. We shall do well to note the conditions that make the fulfillment of the promise possible, conditions that are necessary if we would receive the Holy Spirit in His baptism and abiding.

First, we note that this baptism and

indwelling of the Spirit is only for true disciples, the twice-born, those who are the children of God. Our Lord says with the promise, "The world cannot receive him, because it seeth him not, neither knoweth him." In speaking of the world, it is evident that Jesus is speaking of the unregenerated, those who are not the children of God. So we are to understand, and it would seem no argument is necessary, that sinners, the impenitent, the unbelieving,—the worldly, cannot receive the baptism and abiding of the Holy Spirit. He may and will convince them, if they permit, of sin and all the danger and ruin involved; of righteousness and all the blessings that it can mean, and of the judgment and the fact that we must appear there and receive final sentence. This work belongs to the Holy Spirit and without Him we cannot so illuminate and impress divine truth upon the hearts of the unregenerated that we can produce the desired results, bring them to repentance and to Christ. We must have the presence, activity, illumi-

THE PRESENCE OF GOD 91

nation and conviction wrought by the Holy Spirit in all evangelism that produces good and abiding fruit.

We must call attention to the fact that the disciples who would receive the baptism and abiding of the Holy Spirit must so love Christ that they keep His commandments. The backslidden, the lukewarm, the indifferent never receive the baptism of the Holy Spirit. He is for those who *desire to receive Him*, who love their Lord, and are careful to keep His commandments. He comes upon and remains with those who "hunger and thirst after righteousness," and to such persons we have the pledge and promise of our Lord that they shall be filled, and no doubt they will be filled with the Holy Spirit.

There are those who believe that this promise was only to the twelve, and that it was limited to them, given to them at this time of great need and emergency for the planting of the Christian Church among rejecting Jews and pagan Gentiles. Evidently this is not a correct view. At Pentecost, when the great stir was created among those present from many countries, Peter, preaching the first message he delivered after receiving the Holy Spirit, says to those who are inquiring, "What must we do to be saved?" "Repent, and be baptized every one of you in the name of Jesus Christ for the remission of sins, and ye shall receive the gift of the Holy Ghost. For the promise is unto you, and to your children, and to all that are afar off, even as many as the Lord our God shall call." Acts 2:38, 39.

Peter at once promises the Holy Spirit to every one that repents and believes for pardon, assuring us it was not only for those who were present, but for their children, and those who were as yet afar off who had not heard the message of salvation, and those who might hear in the future, for He says, "Even as many as the Lord our God shall call." Evidently, He means to include those who respond to the call, repent, believe and become the disciples of Christ.

We must not allow ourselves to be-

THE PRESENCE OF GOD

lieve that this gracious promise is shut up to any one class, or to few. It is as broad as the Gospel. It is for every newborn child of God. In His teaching in Luke, 11th chapter, we have a most gracious assurance from Jesus that, "Every one that asketh receiveth; and he that seeketh findeth; and to him that knocketh it shall be opened. If a son shall ask bread of any of you that is a father, will ye give him a stone? or if he ask a fish, will ye for a fish give him a serpent? Or if he shall ask an egg, will ye offer him a scorpion?" How practical and direct are these teachings of our Lord, which He follows immediately with this statement, "If ye then, being evil, know how to give good gifts unto your children: how much more shall your heavenly Father give the Holy Spirit to them that ask him?"

The gift of the Holy Spirit, in His filling and abiding, is for all of the children of God who love Jesus so truly that they keep His commandments and ask the Father for this gracious gift. It is encouraging to note that our Lord said,

"If ye will keep my commandments, I will pray the Father and he will give you another Comforter." So if we love our Lord and keep His commandments we have the assurance that our great Intercessor at the right hand of the Father will pray for us that we may receive the Holy Ghost.

It must not be forgotten that, after the Resurrection, Jesus called the attention of the disciples to this promise which He makes in John 14. It reads thus in the first chapter of Acts: "And, being assembled together with them, commanded them that they should not depart from Jerusalem, but wait for the promise of the Father, which, saith he, ye have heard of me. For John truly baptized with water; but ye shall be baptized with the Holy Ghost not many days hence." This important assurance is added, "Ye shall receive power after that the Holy Ghost is come upon you."

In Matt. 3:11, John, in his preaching, says to the multitude: "I indeed baptize with water unto repentance:

but he that cometh after me is mightier than I, whose shoes I am not worthy to bear; he shall baptize you with the Holy Ghost, and with fire." We do not understand that there is a baptism with fire following the baptism of the Holy Spirit, but that the baptism with the Spirit is a fire purging, consuming, cleansing baptism. Peter tells us, when he speaks of himself and his fellow-disciples who were present on the Day of Pentecost, "Our hearts were purified by faith." The baptism with the Holy Spirit is a cleansing process, a divine fire, which burns up and consumes the carnal nature, brings in and sets up the kingdom of God within the hearts of those who receive Him when He comes to cleanse and abide. John 16:13, 14, reads, "Howbeit when he, the Spirit of truth, is come, he will guide you into all truth: for he shall not speak of himself; but whatsoever he shall hear, that shall he speak: and he will show you things to come. He shall glorify me: for he shall receive of mine, and shall show it unto you."

The baptism with the Holy Spirit is the great conservator of a vital faith in Christ, as revealed in the New Testament Scriptures. We have never heard of any one who had received the baptism with the Holy Spirit who questioned the Virgin Birth of our Lord, the miracles performed by Him as recorded in the New Testament, the redemptive merit of His sufferings upon the cross, or His physical resurrection and ascension into Heaven. Take the modernistic teachers and preachers of the country; none of them claim to have received the baptism with the Holy Spirit, or insist that He shall be sought after or received as an abiding Comforter, teacher, guide, and empowerer for service. Had they received Him they would not be blasting the church with false teaching, destroying the faith of multitudes of people and bringing spiritual paralysis upon the church. Nay, verily, when the Holy Spirit comes upon the child of God who loves the Lord Jesus and keeps His commandments, He glorifies Christ in exalting

THE PRESENCE OF GOD

His pre-existence, His deity and saving power.

One of the serious troubles with the Protestant churches today is that the doctrine of the person of the Holy Spirit and His presence in the world to illuminate, to empower, and to guide in all departments of church work, which is in harmony with the divine plan, has been sadly neglected, and many people might answer, "We have not so much as heard that there be any Holy Spirit." How few sermons are preached in our great city pulpits on the tremendous importance that those who profess salvation and join the church, should seek and obtain the baptism and abiding of the Holy Spirit. Methodist stewards, deacons and elders of other churches, who play golf on the Sabbath day are not hungering and thirsting after righteousness; and multitudes of prominent, influential women who form their bridge clubs and meet at their card parties week after week are not seeking and expecting, neither do they desire, a baptism with the Holy Spirit;

and, according to the plain teachings of Christ, they will not receive Him. It is not at all improbable that these Sunday golfers and bridge players have grieved Him away entirely and are left in darkness, becoming the easy victims of false teachers, wander away after modernistic philosophies and denials of the truth or, go after Eddyism or any other one of the many false doctrines that are proving fatal to many people in the churches, who are untaught, and entirely indifferent to everything concerning our high and holy privileges in spiritual fellowship with Christ in the baptism and abiding with the Holy Spirit who is ever ready to comfort in time of sorrow and distress, to illuminate our pathway through the valley and shadow of death, and to give to us a full assurance as we plume our pinions of faith and love to break out of our captivity here and ascend to our Lord in Paradise.

Saint Paul, in his second letter to the Thessalonians, makes some startling statements with reference to those in

THE PRESENCE OF GOD

the church who are indifferent to the things that are spiritual, who seem to have forgotten what Jesus said to the woman at the well, "God is a spirit, and they that worship him, must worship him in spirit and in truth." No doubt He is slow to anger, plenteous in mercy, but "He will not always chide: neither will he keep his anger forever." The Holy Spirit can be grieved until He takes His departure. In Second Thessalonians, second chapter, Paul speaks of the great deceiver, the man of sin: "Even him, whose coming is after the working of Satan with all power and signs and lying wonders, and with all deceivableness of unrighteousness in them that perish; because they receive not the love of the truth, that they might be saved. And for this cause God shall send them strong delusion, that they should believe a lie: that they all might be damned who believe not the truth, but have pleasure in unrighteousness."

This is a startling statement and easy of comprehension; it reveals the fact that it is very dangerous to trifle with God; to be indifferent to divine truth with all of its requirements and promises; that such a course of conduct prepares one to be led away by the deceiver and that one can refuse to hear the Lord until such one is left of the Lord to be deceived, to be led away by the many false teachers that are paralyzing the church and cursing the world with their suave manners and false teachings which never give any emphasis to the cleansing blood of Christ, or the baptism and incoming of the Holy Spirit to abide as comforter and guide.

And now, my dear reader, how is it with your own soul? Have you received the Holy Spirit since ye believed? Does He abide as your Comforter and empowerer for service? If not, there is a way to insure His coming. Love Christ supremely, keep His commandments, adjust yourself to the divine will, tarry awhile in prayer, and no doubt the blessed Lord will keep His promise and pray the Father for you and you will receive the baptism with the Holy Spirit.

PRAYER.

Our Father in heaven, we do humbly pray that the readers of this message may not toss it aside in indifference, but if they have not received the baptism with the Holy Spirit, may they give themselves at once to such love for our blessed Lord, such obedience to Him, such faith in His atonement and His prayer, that they shall not only trust in Him, but give themselves to prayer, and so hunger and thirst after righteousness, that they shall be filled with righteousness in the gift and blessed abiding of the Holy Spirit. Amen.

IN THE BEGINNING GOD CREATED THE HEAVENS AND THE EARTH.

Genesis 1:1.

(A Commencement sermon preached by the Author at Asbury College)

My subject divides itself under four heads: God in His Universe, God in His Word, God in His Son, and God in His People.

Scientists tell us that somewhere in the past nothing of the material universe as now known had an existence. There was a time when the space now occupied by our globe and all material worlds and spheres was an empty void.

There was a beginning of all material things as they now exist. Our text tells us that God *created*. The Bible does not hesitate to ascribe all matter, as we now have it in the vast realm of material things, to God as its Creator. The Psalmist tuned his harp and sang, "When I consider thy heavens, the work of thy fingers; the moon and the stars, which thou hast ordained; what is man, that thou art mindful of him?" We find the inspired musician attributing the creation of the heavens to God. All through the Scriptures, Old Testament and New, we are taught that the material universe is the building of God.

The vastness of the universe staggers the mind of man. Light travels at the rate of 186,000 miles a second. Astronomers teach us that light traveling from a star of the twelfth magnitude at the rate of 186,000 miles a second cannot reach our planet under thousands of years. This is a staggering thought and with it goes the thought that it takes a great God to create a universe so vast. The harmony with which the planets move, the seasons come and go, the movement of the spheres in the vast fields of space, all bear witness to the greatness of God who has created, arranged, and directed the wonderful order that reigns in this universe so vast that it is entirely beyond the grasp of the human intellect.

Thoughtful men are hardly willing to listen to those who insist that this orderly creation is an accident or that it is governed by chance. The beautiful order, the splendid harmony, the regularity of the seasons, the movement of the spheres, the possibilities of calculating centuries beforehand to the minute the beginning of an eclipse, and the swing in the vast circles of space of the heavenly bodies, confound that skepticism which undertakes to argue and prove that creation is without a creator and brings us back with restful assurance and faith to the truthworthiness of our text, "In the beginning God created the heavens and the earth." The vastness of it bears witness to His omnipotence. The order of it, to His intelligence. The beauty and adaptation of it, to His love. It would seem almost impossible that a man should study the creation, the countless planets, the order and harmony with which they move, and yet remain skeptical and profane. We are not surprised that the greatest scientists and astronomers have been

THE PRESENCE OF GOD

devout and reverential worshippers of the God who is revealed in His universe.

GOD IN HIS WORD

God is revealed to us in His Word. The fulfillment of prophecy is one of the most clear and powerful proofs of the existence of God, His knowledge of the future, and of those things that will take place in the history of the race, and of His power to so communicate to men this knowledge that they can look forward and foretell, with absolute accuracy, events that will take place thousands of years from the time of their prognostication. God has so set the cogs in the wheel of prophecy into the wheel of history, that as we go forward, the movement is so exact and the cogs fit with such accuracy into each other, that we are compelled to believe that there is a supreme and limitless Intelligence that knows the end from the beginning and can reveal that knowledge to men, so that they will write down coming events thousands of years in the future with absolute accuracy and detail.

The Holy Scriptures, Old Testament and New, contain prophecy in fulfilling of such remarkable character that it lifts the Word of God out of the realm of mere human knowledge and stamps it as a divinely inspired Book, a gracious revelation of divine truth from that great Being of whom the inspired writer wrote when he said, "In the beginning God created the heavens and the earth."

GOD IN HIS SON

The revelation of God in His Son is the crown and triumph of all miracles. It is the central sun of all revelation. It is the wonder of men and angels that God in His Son, in the form of a man, should have come into the world, combining in this one Person the humanity that could hunger, thirst, weep, and die, and the Deity that could triumph over all the weaknesses and frailties of humanity, and conquer death. No doubt the world needed a human-divine Christ; a humanity that could suffer with men; a high priest who could be tempted in every point, even as man is tempted, and a divinity that could conquer all temptations, break the power and force of all evil, and triumph for himself and others over every possible foe.

Our Lord Jesus Christ, God in the flesh, could hunger like a man, but like a God He could bless and break a few little loaves, and feed to fullness, the multiplied thousands of hungry people. Like a weary man, He could sleep quietly in the ship tossed by the tempest, and, on awakening, like a human being he could rub the drowsiness out of His eyes, and say like God, to the tempest, "Peace, be still," and at once the winds cease to blow and the waves sink into calmness. Like a man, Christ could weep at the grave of his friend, Lazarus, and like God He could command the dead to arise and at once Lazarus arises and walks forth in his graveclothes. Like a man, He could sit down at the table and eat with sinners, and like God, he could say to a penitent, "Your sins are all forgiven; go in peace and sin no more." Like a man, He could hang bleeding and dying upon the cross; and like God, He could say to a guilty thief, "This day shalt thou be with me in Paradise." Like a man, He could die in the midst of the ridicule and and mockery of the mob; like a compassionate God who so loved the world that He gave His Son, He could plead for mercy for those who nailed Him upon the cross. Like a man, He could be buried. Like a God, He could arise, forsake the tomb, and stand in the calm majesty of His creative power and say, "All power is given unto me in heaven and in earth."

Men never could have understood God in the fullness of His compassionate nature and love if He had not been revealed in Jesus Christ, His Son, who came and taught us when we pray to say, "Our Father, who art in heaven." It was Jesus who revealed to us the fact that this Creator of the vast universe is so conscious of everything that transpires that not a sparrow falls without His notice. Jesus reached the highest climax of the fatherly love of God in the parable of the prodigal son, when he represents the sinner going to the farthest limits of degradation and ruin; he is at the point to perish; and he turns his weary, staggering steps back toward the father's house in humble confession and readiness to be received simply as a servant. But the watchful father sees him in the distance, runs to meet him, receives him in his arms with repeated kisses, removes his rags and clothes him with a robe, places shoes upon his feet, the covenant ring of his love upon his finger, and prepares a feast of rejoicing that the lost is found, the dead is alive. How wonderful the truth of the divine nature revealed in this parable; it ought to bring a sinful world to repentance, to saving faith, and devout worship with joyful praise. God reveals Himself in the creation of His universe, in the inspiration of His Word, in the life, teachings, death, and resurrection of His Son.

GOD IN HIS PEOPLE

The revelations which we have mentioned are not the end in the mind of God. They are means to an end. He has thus revealed Himself that He might make an additional, a supreme revelation. He would now reveal Himself to men and in men. So far as the teachings of the Bible are concerned, the chief aim and end of God is to get Himself revealed to men and, by divine grace and power, into men and through those in whom He dwells to reveal Himself to all men.

Let us imagine a great man, a captain of industry; he owns a system of railroads; he owns great sea-going ships; he owns factories; he is the president of a system of banks; his business interests reach out over the seas; he controls centers of commerce in many nations; he has vast wealth; he employs great armies of workers; the best trained experts are at his command; he has the best legal talent in various countries; and he is going forward with enterprises and vast income; he has ac-

THE PRESENCE OF GOD 111

cumulated an art gallery of the paintings of the most famous artists; he has a museum filled with relics of the past and the inventions of modern science; his mind is occupied with many things; he has a little son; the son is the image of his father; he carries his father's name; he's an only child; he is to inherit his father's fortune, carry forward his enterprises, and distribute his charities. He's the darling of his father's heart, the hope of his future. The father knows that by and by he will grow old and in the end must die, but he goes forward with ever renewed interest in his work because he feels sure that his son will take his place.

The child is taken sick. He grows worse. The most skillful physicians are called in, great specialists are hurried in airships. No expense is spared. He is ready to give his all if he can save that son. Losing that son, he has largely lost interest in all of his enterprises.

The Scriptures lead us to believe that this man would be something like God.

He has tremendous enterprises. His resources are beyond the possibility of mathematics to calculate. In the evening he says, "Attention!" and millions of stars wheel into line and illuminate the skies and baptize the earth with their mellow glow. In the morning, he says, "March!" and more than fifty millions of suns move out in order through boundless space in obedience to the voice of their Creator and Commander. There is no way to calculate the vast possessions, resources, and interests of the great God of this universe. But man is sick. He is sinful. He is lost. He is moving toward the abyss. Eternal darkness is ahead of him. And God seems to forget everything else; all other worlds of His creation are left to run their course; and He centers His thought and activities upon this prodigal child of His. Prophets are hurried into activity. Angels' wings that mock the lightning's flight rush down from heaven. All creation groans with sympathy and desire to save this sin-sick child which God has created in His own image to inherit and enjoy his vast estates. Experts have examined the situation and there is no way to save him except a blood transfusion. New life must be infused into him. That of bullocks is not sufficient. The blood of all the bleating lambs of all the world cannot remove the disease of sin which is eating into the vitals of his soul. The blood of all the men that have died on the battlefields in all the wars of human history cannot remove the stain.

There is only one that can wash away the foul spot upon the soul of man, and that is the sinless Son of God, who has lived and reigned in the bosom of the Father since before the dawn of human history, before there was one atom or electron of the vast physical universe. No poet in song could describe the love of the Father and the Son. In the vast eternity of the past they have been one. No orator could ever picture the flow of affection between those two beings alike in eternal existence, omnipotent power, infinite love, and holy oneness.

But an hour has come, a tragic moment in history. What's to be done? The human race is lost, is marching into doom and darkness. God gives His Son. Jesus steps forth in the majesty of His almightiness and gives Himself in agony and blood. Its cleansing power removes the stain. The sin-sick soul rises in health, holiness, and happiness. The angels shout. The earth rejoices. The great God has come to the rescue and has paid the price. We find that this is the great end toward which we have been moving in that vast background of history of which we know so little. He set Himself to redeem mankind, to bring back the prodigal to His embrace, to bring reconciliation between Himself and a sinful race.

When it comes to the salvation of man, it seems that God was a bit hard to satisfy. He is intensely interested. He must win the heart completely. He must know that man is all His own. Nothing will please God short of absolute surrender and at last entire consecration, a heart from sin set free, and the setting up of His Kingdom within the heart of man. The Apostle tells us

THE PRESENCE OF GOD

the Kingdom of God is not "meat and drink, but righteousness, peace, and joy in the Holy Ghost." Again, he says, "The Kingdom of God is within you."

Electricity is about us everywhere. It is not understood. Edison himself could not explain it. He could tell us of its uses, but that's another point. It is invisible. It is powerful. It can come upon you with the suddenness of lightning. It can pass through your body quicker than thought and may destroy disease germs and renew your physical life.

The Holy Spirit, the blessed Third Person of the divine Trinity, is invisible, but He is here. He is about us everywhere. He is omnipresent and He can be poured upon us in a divine baptism, penetrating, powerful as an electric current, destroying sin, sanctifying soul and spirit, and bringing us into blessed harmony with the Holy Trinity.

The atonement made by Jesus Christ makes abundant provision for the entire sin problem. Transgressions may be pardoned, the stains of sin may be cleansed away, the old man, the carnal nature may be crucified and, "being made free from sin, we become servants to God, have our fruit unto holiness, and the end everlasting life."

This is the foundation upon which we build here at Asbury College. This is our faith. On this we risk the destiny of our immortal souls in a boundless universe in an unending eternity.

In the Beginning God. God in His universe. God in His Word. God in His Son. God in His people.

PRAYER.

Our Divine Father, grant that we may know thee, the true God, and Jesus Christ whom thou hast sent into the world to save sinners. May we so live that our lives shall show forth the beauty of His holiness, that men may take notice of us that we have been with Jesus and learned of Him. May thy Holy Spirit so indwell us, that we may be living epistles known and read of men, thus leading them to accept the Lamb of God who taketh away the sin of the world. This we ask in His name, and for His sake. Amen.

THE CRUCIFIXION

"Today shalt thou be with me in Paradise." Luke 23:43.

There has never been invented a more cruel and painful method of inflicting the death penalty than that which was inflicted by the Romans—crucifixion upon a wooden cross. The victim was nailed with a spike in each hand sufficient to bear his weight upon a cross beam; the feet were placed, one above the other, so that a heavy spike could pierce them both into the upright beam of the cross, which was then placed in a socket prepared in the earth, and the victim was lifted up, exposed to the public gaze, and kept there until he died a most painful death. The wounds in the hands and feet were such that there was little blood letting; the nails largely closed the rents made in the hands and feet of the victim. They sometimes lived quite a while under the blazing sun or freezing cold. Wherever the Roman eagle went in the conquest of the world, the cross went for the torture of those that Roman officials chose to sentence to death, and hand over to the public executioner.

Rome had supreme power over Palestine in the days of Christ's ministry. The death sentence belonged to them alone; the Jews had no power to execute a prisoner; had they had this power no doubt they would have slain Jesus by stoning; several times they were so indignant at His ministry and His claims to be the Son of God that they picked up stones to stone Him. Being bereft of this power they constantly sought to bring Jesus into conflict with Roman authorities, and they finally succeeded in bringing him before Pilate, chief executive of Roman authority, with an accusation that Jesus deserved death. It was a mock trial. Pilate, the judge, admitted that "he found no fault in the man." He turned into a defendant, rather than a judge, and was eager to release Jesus; but when some one in the mob cried out, "If thou let this man go,

THE PRESENCE OF GOD 119

thou art not Cæsar's friend," his political fears were aroused. He loved office; if it were reported to Cæsar that he had released a man who admitted that he was King of the Jews and a man so beloved by the common people that they were ready to take Him by force and make him King it would no doubt give him very bad standing before Cæsar. Pilate had a sense of justice and believed Jesus to be innocent; that "for envy the Jews had delivered him." He had his superstitious fears, for his wife had sent some one who had tip-toed through the throng and whispered in his ear, "Have nothing to do with this just man for I have suffered many things of him today in a dream."

So his sense of justice and his superstitious fears would have released Jesus, but his political ambitions, when this cry from the mob, "If thou let this man go, thou art not Cæsar's friend," at once decided him; he passed the death sentence and turned Jesus over to a group of soldiers for execution, who scourged Him, and you may be sure that was severe torture; then they mocked Him, spit upon Him, smote Him. It's a fearful scene to look upon, however, it should not be forgotten, and we shall do well to contemplate this scene. It should bow us in humility, it should stir within us a deep appreciation of the price paid for our redemption; it ought to chasten us, to bring to us a deep and holy awe, produce in us a detestation of sin, to appreciate the love that gave so innocent a Victim to suffer such agony that we might be saved. It ought to make us tremble at the thought of rejecting such a Saviour.

It occurs to me that those who have heard the gospel preached, who have known the way of salvation, who have had offered to them the Christ, and who have spurned the offer, and who are lost at last, will have a pang of pain deeper than the torture of the fires of hell, a vivid abiding memory of a rejected Saviour. God forbid that any who reads this should have to carry such a memory through the ceaseless ages of eternity; a night of darkness without a star

THE PRESENCE OF GOD 121

of hope or the grey of morning dawn to alleviate their sorrow.

On the wing of thought let us visit the tragic scene in Jerusalem at the time of the crucifixion. There are three victims on crosses: Jesus in the midst, with a robber on either hand. Roman soldiers are there to see that the death penalty is inflicted and to prevent any outbreak; the mob is there with its hunger for the blood of the innocent Christ. We do not read that any one reproached the robbers or cast indignant ridicule upon them in their dying agony; but they did heap their reproaches upon the thorn-crowned, beaten, spitted upon, suffering Man of Galilee. There, perhaps, had been nothing like it in the history of the world. The dignitaries of the church were there looking on with satisfaction, feeling that at last, they are saving Israel, and they challenge the dying Christ to prove His Messiahship by coming down from the cross. How satisfactory that challenge appears to them; they shout with glee, "He saved others, himself he cannot save." Mary, with the devout, brokenhearted women, hears these words of challenge and mockery with a painful agony that no tongue could utter and no pen could write. John, the beloved disciple, is standing there; he, like the suffering women, is speechless. Jesus wills his mother, no doubt a poor widow, to the care of John. Dear man, his heart is ready to burst with an agony of love and pity at the strange and awful mystery of this darkest hour in human history. I can imagine him looking up to Jesus with silent lips and pleading eyes that say, "Master, don't die. Thou hast calmed the ocean storm; thou hast healed disease; thou hast raised the dead; prove thy identity as the Son of God by coming down from the cross. So display thy power before the ecclesiasticisms, the Roman soldiers, the shouting mob, and mocking, curious multitude that no one can doubt but thou art the Son of God."

That Jesus could have done this, there is no doubt. A little while ago He had asserted that He could call more

THE PRESENCE OF GOD

than twelve legions of angels to His rescue. He could have made the earth open her mouth and swallow up the Roman army, priests and accusers, the shouting mob and mocking crowd. He could have glorified Himself before them in garments whiter than the light, and ascended into heaven. But He did none of these things. He gave Himself, the sacrificial Lamb of God, to die for the redemption of the world.

It appears that the two victims crucified, one on the right and the other on the left hand of Jesus, were not sneak thieves, but robbers, the worst type of criminals. Thieves sneak about under the cover of darkness and slyly seize what they can lay their hands on; but robbers come upon you, prepared not only to take your substance, money, jewelry, or whatever you may possess, but your life also. They are desperate men; such men are dominated by the vilest lusts; they have no reverence for the aged, nor pity for women and children. They have thrown away the bridle of restraint and given themselves to greedy, daring selfishness that hesitates at no crime. They are the worst of men.

One of these robbers joined with the Jews and the mob in his abuse of the Christ, and repeats the challenge of those who mocked our dying Lord. "If thou be the Son of God, save thyself and us." The other rebukes him; no doubt looking across at his suffering comrade in crime, said, "Dost not thou fear God, seeing thou art in the same condemnation? And we indeed justly; for we receive the due reward of our deeds: but this man hath done nothing amiss."

This was the only plea made for Jesus as He suffered there for our redemption. Note that this robber had come to himself. He appears to be surprised at the rashness of his comrade in crime. "Dost thou not fear God?" he asked. Evidently, the fear of God had come into his heart. He is a penitent; he admits his guilt. "We receive the due reward of our deeds." This is a humble and deep confession. Then, no doubt, he turned his head and glanced to the

THE PRESENCE OF GOD

Christ, and added, "But this man hath done nothing amiss." It is reasonable to suppose that at this word of warning to his fellow criminal, this confession of guilt and this word of testimony to the innocence of Jesus, that Jesus turned and looked at him. I have always believed that their eyes met each other, and that there came into this penitent, confessing robber a flash of truth. Repentance and confession of sin open the windows of the soul and let in the light of truth. At once, he says, and says it with genuine faith, "Lord, remember me when thou comest into thy kingdom."

A mountain of guilt was upon him, hell was beneath him, and there was salvation near, a mighty Saviour hanging there in blood and agony. He dares to lift up a cry for mercy. Thank God, his cry is heard. At once the answer comes to him. Jesus demonstrates to the mocking priests and Roman soldiers who have scourged, smitten, spit upon and thorn-crowned Him, that He is the Son of God, with power to forgive sins, mighty to save. They may put mock robes upon Him, place a crown of thorns upon His head, blaspheme and ridicule Him, but they cannot take away from Him His Godhead, His oneness with the Father, His power to save from sin. His gracious answer comes; let it never be forgotten; let it be repeated over and over to the guilty multitudes; let it be carried as a last word of hope to the prisoner's cell before he goes to execution; let it be whispered with faith in the ear of a dying sinner before he takes his last, long leap into eternity. Let us remember these words of our blessed Lord to the dying criminal, and come into a more intense love and devotion to Him who bore our sins upon the cross. "And Jesus said unto him, Verily I say unto thee, today, shalt thou be with me in Paradise."

These were the last words our Lord uttered to a human being before his death. "It was about the sixth hour, and there was darkness over all the earth until the ninth hour. And the sun was darkened, and the veil of the temple was rent in the midst. And when Jesus had cried with a loud voice, He said, Father, into thy hands I commend my spirit: And having said thus, he gave up the ghost." There is this significant verse in the history of this tragedy upon which we may well reflect, "And all the people that came together to that sight, beholding the things that were done, smote their breasts, and returned."

No doubt there was something in all this suffering of Christ, this cry of the penitent, and this ready response in the promise of salvation, that profoundly impressed the people. These words are significant; "They smote their breasts." When I hear of men claiming to be preachers of the gospel, or sitting in chairs in seminaries teaching young ministers how to go forth and preach, denying that Jesus was the pre-existent Son of God, that His teachings were, and are, eternal truth; that His death upon Calvary provided an atonement for the sins of all those who repent and come to him in faith for salvation; that, even to this late day, we have men in the church, many of whom join with the accusers of the Christ, denying His Godhead and redemptive power, I, too, feel like smiting upon my breast, with a surprised horror and wondering that it is possible for an institution claiming to be the Church of God, should employ and pay large salaries to such blasphemers of our redeeming Christ.

We can but feel the profoundest respect for this man "Joseph, a counsellor; and he was a good man and a just." He goes to Pilate, "And begs the body of Jesus." It has been a means of grace to me, in my imagination, to stand with the sorrowing group, as they take Jesus down from the cross, and stretch his limp body; the women who loved Him gather about; with tears, they wipe the blood from His wounds; they look into that serene, quiet, holy face, which had beamed upon them with such heavenly light and love. They cannot understand! How mysterious it all is! But they continue to love, and doubtless, in their sorrow there is a hope. How tenderly they wrap the body with the spices which had been prepared, and lay Him in the near-by tomb cut in the solid rock, and quietly, with heavy hearts, they return to their desolate homes.

I can imagine some one saying, "I saw a strange light flash through the sky. Perhaps it was lightning out of the dark clouds which shrouded the heavens; it may be the gleam of a far away comet, in its rapid flight." It was neither. It was Jesus in the chariot of God going home to Paradise with a redeemed sinner caught from the very verge of the pits of doom. Of course, the inhabitants of Paradise know that Jesus is coming. Preparation is made for His reception; the choirs of heaven have gathered into one vast throng; the gallery in which they sit will hold its millions; they are able to carry all the parts with trained voices that echo through the vaults of glory. I see the great leader of the singing hosts come out, with his golden baton, and then begin in deep and measured tones, "Lift up your heads, O ye gates; even lift them up, ye everlasting doors, and the King of glory shall come in."

Evidently, heaven was well acquainted with the tragedy taking place on earth. Moses and Elias had talked with Christ upon the mount of the death he should accomplish in Jerusalem, and with this mighty song of welcome, Jesus walks into Paradise to the shouts of the saved millions, and the songs of countless angels; but by His side there is a man who, a few moments ago, was a robber doomed to eternal night; but now, he is white as snow. What a triumph! What a splendid victory over an apostate church, the Roman legions and the mocking mob, who cried through the streets, "Let him be crucified!"

Let it be known through all the earth, and to all the guilty souls of sinful men, that Jesus is the same yesterday, today and forever, mighty to save to the uttermost. As we turn from these scenes of the agonies of the cross, the hatred of an apostate church and the shouts of the mob, let us weep with grief over human sinfulness. Let us, with a deeper devotion, a more complete consecration and a higher faith, worship our Lord, and determine to spread His gospel to the world, and make it our mission to carry the good news to the most sinful, degraded and hopeless human beings, that there is salvation for those who cry to Christ for mercy. Let us seek the prodigal who has wandered farthest from his father's house, who is deepest in degradation and despair, and assure him that an anxious Father waits with open arms of compassion and a joyful welcome to all who will return with penitence, however numerous and deep the dye of their sins. Let us insist and repeat it, that "Jesus Christ by the grace of God, hath tasted death for every man," and that He has declared that, "Whosoever cometh unto me, I will in no wise cast out."

PRAYER

Our heavenly Father, grant that all who may read this message, may have a deep appreciation of the price that was paid for their redemption from sin; and grant that each one may know this Christ, mighty to save to the uttermost, all who come unto God by Him. God forbid, that any one who reads this message should be eternally lost, and that the blood of Calvary's Victim should have been shed in vain for them. May the sacrifice made on Calvary give us a horror for sin and a love for holiness, for "without holiness no man can be saved." This we ask in Jesus' name. Amen.

ENTIRE SANCTIFICATION

"Knowing this, that our old man is crucified with (Christ,) that the body of sin might be destroyed, that henceforth we should not serve sin." Rom. 6:6. *"But now being made free from sin, and become servants to God, ye have your fruit unto holiness, and the end everlasting life."* Rom. 6:22.

The Scriptures speak of the mystery of iniquity. There is no more profound mystery in this world, and this life of ours, than the sin problem. We find sin as universal as the human race. There has not been found a nation, a tribe, an isolated group of islanders, or a family in all the history of the world who were in, and of, themselves, holy.

Sin has stained and befouled the fountain stream of human life. We find it everywhere. Its origin, the sorrow and wreckage it has wrought among mankind, have claimed the deepest thought of the most profound philosophers; how it originated and continues its wide sweep of merciless ruin among men is an unsolved and mysterious problem when left alone for human solution.

When we turn to the Bible it, without hesitation, gives us the simple story of the origin of sin. God created human beings pure, upright and beautiful. They were the happy associates of their Creator before they listened to the tempter's seductive voice, or sin had stamped its vile insignia upon their spotless spirits. Mother Eve, the original woman, is charged with the first offense, with opening the floodgates from which the ever widening and deepening river of human depravity, with all of its fearful results, has flowed.

Before we charge Mother Eve too severely for her unfortunate act, we must remember that she knew nothing of the nature and fearful effects of sin. She had seen no sinners; there had never existed a staggering drunkard; a woman blasted by low and vulgar sin had not existed. A little child, diseased and wrecked from birth by the sins of its

THE PRESENCE OF GOD 135

parents, was unknown. There had been no crash of war and battlefields strewn with dead and wounded. Had Mother Eve understood the meaning of sin, and the ruin it would bring upon the race, the liquor traffic with its blasted millions, war with its blood and fire, no doubt she would have resisted the tempter and kept the divine commandments.

Perhaps the same is true of all of us. If we could see and understand the far-reaching and blighting effect of the sins we have committed before we committed them, the strong probabilities are we would have resisted the tempter and like our Christ, would have said, "Get thee behind me, Satan." But there's the rub! We stumble about in our ignorance, neglect duty without understanding the dire effect, the life that might have been useful is wasted, the soul that might have been saved is lost; a handshake, a few kindly words, and eye glazed with the tear of sympathy, a tremor in the voice, with words of entreaty, could have changed the whole trend and current of a life and made a minister of the gospel who might have won thousands of souls to Christ, and started the sowing of seed that would have reproduced itself to the coming of the Lord, but we neglected our opportunity; we were slow and stupid and hardly thought of our indifference, while we comforted our poor selves that we were saved, meanwhile had little conception of duty and opportunity. It must be remembered there are sins of omission as well as sins of commission. Who of us cannot recall how that some human being was instrumental in our salvation: remembering this, we should be active in the harvest field of lost souls.

The question has been asked, "Why did not God create human beings so they could not sin?" It was impossible to create intelligent beings capable of reason, of education and development fitted for the sphere for which God created man, without the possibility of sinning. An idiot, born without the faculties of reason, who has no will power to understand or to choose between good and evil, cannot sin; he is not responsible for his acts, however hurtful or unfortunate they may be; but God did not want a race of idiots. He desired an intelligent being that was capable of thinking, endowed with reasoning power, of taking the things that God had given him, combining them, developing them, and bringing them to the highest possible perfection. It is interesting to note that, in nature, there are many hints of the possibilities, and man is so endowed that he can take those hints and bring out marvelous, and beautiful results. Most all grains, vegetables, fruits and flowers, as well as animals, are capable of crossings, culture and development far beyond the original species. It is the delight of a parent to give a child blocks, figures, playthings, capable of certain adjustments to bring them into a harmonious whole, and watch the young mind as it thinks and labors until it is able to make the proper combination.

So it is with our heavenly Father.

When we look about us we see the remarkable inventions wrought by man; the things we once thought impossible have become commonplace. How marvelous the whole realm of scientific discovery and development, with perhaps, nothing having reached absolute perfection, or a place where there is not the possibility of improvment. As we meditate on these things our hearts are warmed with an adoration to God and we are thankful that He did not give us perfected things, but materials, minds and longings which have enabled us to labor through the millenniums and centuries discovering and developing, until we have surrounded ourselves with many agencies and comforts that we once thought quite impossible.

A being that could not sin, that had not the power of reasoning and choice, would have been entirely out of harmony with the divine plan and purpose. What if sin had not broken in upon the race. Suppose if, from the first, there had been no sin; if from Adam and Eve the race had been obedient to the divine commandments and lived in fellowship with God, what marvelous progress the race would have made; what physical perfection; what mental capacity; what purity of heart; what a perfect social system would have obtained; what freedom from disease; what marvelous progress in all the sciences, the combination and development of the materials with which God has supplied us.

Along down through history there have appeared persons with remarkable endowments; gifts bestowed upon them born with, and in, them which they did not seek nor strive to cultivate. It seemed natural for them to do things. Some years ago, we had in Kentucky a negro with limited education who was a born mathematician; he could almost instantly solve any problem you proposed. If you stood with him looking at a train, you could say, "Bill, that car wheel is so many feet, so many inches and so many fractions of an inch in circumference. It is so many miles, so many feet, so many inches and so many fractions of an inch from here to Central Station, Boston, Mass. How many times will that car wheel have to turn to reach the end of the track in Boston?" Almost instantly, he could give the accurate answer, proven by those who figured out the facts and found him correct. I have a son who has taught in the high schools in Ohio. In one of his classes he had a boy that had this remarkable gift as a mathematician. But for the fall, we might all have had that gift and not been compelled to puzzle our brains over multiplication tables. Ole Bull could play the violin with such marvelous enchantment and power that vast audiences were fairly mesmerized. They forgot their enmities, their grudges; they forgot their troubles; they forgot the burden of their debts; they forgot the diseases that preyed upon their bodies, the sorrows that darkened their lives; they listened, they wept, their souls caught fire. But for sin, we might all have been able to finger the strings and draw the bow so that the world would re-

THE PRESENCE OF GOD

sound with harmonious music. Blind Tom, born sightless, and practically an idiot, when a little boy got into his master's parlor, got his fingers on the keyboard of the piano and startled the family with charming music. He became one of the wonders of the world. He could imitate perfectly, anything he ever heard, from lullaby music, with gentle touch to hush a babe to sleep, or the thunder of cannon, the charge of cavalry and the clash of swords in battle. But for sin, it may be that all of us would have had these gifts, or at least, some gift in its perfection. When Jenny Lind came to this country she sang with such beauty that no opera house was large enough to hold the crowds that longed to hear the sweet notes of her charming voice. Her power over an audience was marvelous. No doubt sin has so affected our capacity for song that we of the multitudes fall far beneath what would have been possible to us.

I have never heard any one play the

violin that I did not feel within that I could surpass the player, if I could play as well as the player played. I have heard no one sing that I did not feel I could lift the note a little higher and give it a more tender and pathetic softness if I had the power to sing as well as the singer to whom I listened. It was this inward urge, this spiritual stir within me, this consciousness of imperfection, of the possibilities of something better, that led me to compose on my sick bed one night, the little poem:

I cannot sing like I long to sing,
   Like I shall sing by and by,
When my captive spirit breaks its bars
   And I ascend beyond the stars.

I cannot speak one tenth I feel
   While tramelled with this clod;
But I will speak my heart's full praise,
   When I ascend to God.

I cannot rest, like I long to rest,
   My body racked with pain;
But oh, I'll rest the sweetest rest,
   When Paradise I gain.

Ah, Satan, thou once high and mighty angel, how bereft of all possibility or capacity for good or joy, thou enemy of God and humanity, beyond the wreckage which thou hast wrought; the disease and sickness thou hast brought to humanity; the drunkenness and degradation that has blasted and dost continue to blast countless millions of homes and the almost ceaseless war of blood and fire and untold suffering through the centuries; and if thou wast capable of sorrow, then thou wouldst hide away to darkest recesses and the lowest pits of hell, and contemplate with unutterable sorrow through the long night of eternity the wretchedness thou hast brought to humanity in thy war against God and all that He has created and loved.

The Bible declares that all have sinned. We accept the declaration and accusation without hesitation. Sin's fearful stain is on all the race. We find it in the babe long before it understands anything about the laws of good or evil, and the penalties attached for wrong-doing. The child naturally does wrong before it is accountable, or responsible for the wrong it does. With its natural tendencies to evil, the only possibility of saving it from crime, is discipline, the guidance of kindly mind and strong hand, the wise infliction of punishment for wrong-doing. It is the lack of discipline in the home and in the school that has brought upon us the thousands of criminals who, having been left to the evil tendencies within them, have developed into heartless gangsters in the immature years of youth.

Depravity, selfishness, the spirit of revenge, the strong inclination to the indulgence of the desires of the flesh, possess the entire race. There is no offer of hope or promise of salvation to any human being apart from repentance, faith in Christ and the change of the spiritual nature so deep and radical that Jesus calls it a new birth, a regeneration, a re-creation, a new creature.

John tells us that "If we confess our sins, he is faithful and just to forgive us our sins, and to cleanse us from all unrighteousness." In bringing the soul back into its original purity and fellowship with its God, there are two gracious works of grace that are necessary: One is the pardoning of transgressions and the incoming of a new life; the other is the cleansing away, the outgoing of an old life. Our text calls it the "Crucifixion of the old man." The destruction of the body of sin; an inward principle that is carnal, that is not subject to the law of God, neither indeed, can be. A strange something spoken of in the Scriptures that is antagonistic to divine law, to spiritual life, to cheerful obedience to God. A something that cannot be regenerated or educated into glad obedience to the divine commandment and will, but opposes itself to all of our best desires, purposes and emotions; that hinders and hurts the best that has come into us by the regenerating power of the Holy Spirit. Whatever St. Paul may have meant in the seventh of Romans, and whatever the gracious possibilities of the regenerated life may be, who of us has not felt at times a war 'within our members,' uprisings which sometimes have broken out in action so that we could sadly say, "When I would do good, evil is present with me."

It would be difficult to exaggerate a description of the degradation of the carnal mind and its capabilities, if unbridled and unrestrained and turned loose to the fulfillment of all of its corrupt desires.

Our Lord Jesus, speaking of the natural state of the human heart, says: "For from within, out of the heart of men, proceed evil thoughts, adulteries, fornications, murders, thefts, covetousness, wickedness. deceit, lasciviousness, an evil eye, blasphemy, pride, foolishness; all these evil things come from within, and defile the man." St. Paul in his epistle to the Galatians, gives us a fearful picture of the sinful condition of a human being, and the conflict between the flesh, that is, the sinful nature, and the Spirit of God. It reads like this: "For the flesh lusteth against the Spirit." We must remember that

Paul is not telling us that there is any war between the meat on a man's bones and the soul within his body, or the Holy Spirit. The word *flesh* stands for that same old man in our text. He continues: "And the Spirit against the flesh, and these are contrary one to the other; so that ye cannot do the things that ye would. But if ye be led of the Spirit, ye are not under the law. For the works of the flesh (carnal nature, old man) are manifest, which are these: adultery, fornication, uncleanness, lasciviousness, idolatry, witchcraft, hatred, variance, emulations, wrath, strife, seditions, heresies, envyings, murders, drunkenness, revellings, and such like: of which I tell you before, as I have told you in time past, that they which do such things shall not inherit the kingdom of God." Paul draws the contrast and tells us that "The fruit of the Spirit is love, joy, peace, longsuffering, gentleness, goodness, faith, meekness, temperance; against such there is no law. And they that are Christ's have crucified the flesh with the affections and lusts."

We do not understand the Apostle Paul in this description he gives of the flesh or the carnal nature, the old man, to intimate that the re-born, the child of God, is under the domination of the carnal nature. It is understood that the new life imparted in regeneration not only enables the child of God to resist the temptation of Satan and his emissaries, but also gives him the mastery over the uprisings of remaining sin, the carnal nature, which has not yet been crucified. It should be understood that there is a difference between *sins* which are committed and are to be pardoned, and *sin* which is inherited and must be cleansed away, or in the language of the text, is denominated as the "old man" who is not to be disposed of by forgiveness, but is to be crucified in order that the body, the inbeing, the sinful carnal mind, which is not subject to the law of God, neither can be, may be cleansed away.

Sins committed bring guilt calling for forgiveness; sin inherited brings defilement which must be cleansed away. In the gracious work of pardon one is justified and regenerated; a new life comes into those who receive forgiveness; something the penitent believer never had before. It is a new birth, a re-creation. In sanctification an old life, a sinful principle, the body of sin, that strange something that is always anti-God, is cleansed away.

Sanctification received subsequent to regeneration involves a baptism with the Holy Spirit; this baptism with the Spirit, as we are plainly taught by our Lord Jesus in the fourteenth chapter of John, verses 15, 16, 17, can be received only by those who have been regenerated. The words of the Lord are very plain. We read: "If ye love me, keep my commandments. And I will pray the Father and he shall give you another Comforter, that he may abide with you forever; even the Spirit of truth; whom the world cannot receive, because it seeth him not, neither knoweth him: but ye know him; for he dwelleth with you, and shall be in you."

We understand that the Spirit of truth in the teaching of our Lord means the Holy Spirit who is promised to those who love Him so truly and genuinely that they keep His commandments. This represents a gracious state of the justified child of God who gladly keeps the commandment of the Christ he loves; not out of fear of the evil consequences that might accrue, but out of a devoted love for Christ. We understand in our Lord's use of the word world, when He says, "whom the world cannot receive," that He refers to the unregenerated, the sinner, those who are in rebellion against God. "The whole world lieth in wickedness." The word world has no reference to the earth on which we live, but the unsaved who live upon the earth.

There has been much hurtful confusion with reference to the baptism with the Holy Spirit. Some have taught that, after receiving sanctification through the cleansing blood of Christ, there is a definite baptism with the Holy Spirit. This teaching is unfortu-

THE PRESENCE OF GOD

nate and has been the occasion of no little confusion and hurtful fanaticism among devout people who, if properly taught, would have been sane and safe. Entire sanctification is a gracious work wrought by a baptism with the Holy Spirit destroying the carnal nature, crucifying the old man, eradicating the sinful nature and coming in to abide as comforter, teacher, guide and empowerer for service.

It is the privilege of every child of God to have the carnal nature removed; the old man crucified, the body of sin destroyed, that now "being made free from sin, and become servants to God, ye have your fruit unto holiness, and the end everlasting life." This gracious work was wrought in the disciples of our Lord, with the devout believers assembled with them in the upper room, on the day of Pentecost when the Holy Spirit fell upon them, Peter afterward testifying that, "Our hearts were purified by faith." Those who oppose the cleansing away of the "body of sin" by a baptism with the Holy Spirit, and who undertake to prove that the disciples had not been converted prior to Pentecost, must labor in vain. Our Lord sent them out to preach with power, to cast out devils, to heal the sick, sometime prior to Pentecost. When they rejoiced that the devils were subject unto them, He told them to rejoice because their names were written in the Lamb's book of life.

In that remarkable prayer just before His arrest, in John 17, our Lord Jesus says to the Father, with reference to His disciples, "I pray for them: I pray not for the world." He is mentioning the fact that this prayer is not being offered for the unregenerate and sinful, "But for them which thou hast given me; for they are thine. All mine are thine, and thine are mine; and I am glorified in them." He continues, "While I was with them in the world, I kept them in thy name: those whom thou hast given me I have kept, and none of them is lost, but the son of perdition; that the Scriptures might be fulfilled. And now I come to thee; and these things I speak in the world, that they might have my joy fulfilled in themselves. I have given them thy word; and the world hath hated them, because they are not of the world, even as I am not of the world."

It would seem that this teaching in the prayer of our Lord would make it clear to any mind that is not darkened by prejudice, that the disciples were in a regenerated state before Pentecost. We do not find Jesus praying the Father to forgive them, but every utterance in the prayer makes it clear that they were not of the world, and that they were so separated from the world that the world hated them; moreover, the Lord declares most positively, that "none of them is lost." If they were not lost, and Jesus says they were not, they were saved. The Holy Spirit never comes in sanctifying power upon the unregenerated and those in rebellion against God. This abundant grace, this gracious experience vouchsafed by St. Peter in his memorable sermon at Pentecost, in which he said, "The promise is unto you and your children, and all those who are afar off, even as many as the Lord our God shall call," is vouchsafed to every child of God having been born again, and now loving your Lord with a love that makes obedience a joy, you are a proper subject and have a right, by consecration and faith, to receive a baptism with the Holy Spirit by which the old man is crucified and the body of sin destroyed, that henceforth, ye should not serve sin. "But now being made free from sin, and become servants to God, ye have your fruit unto holiness, and the end everlasting life."

PRAYER

Our Father in heaven, we do humbly pray that thy Spirit may illuminate and guide anyone who may read this message, and that if such an one has not received the Holy Spirit in sanctifying power, such one may be led to seek, to consecrate, to believe and receive Him in the crucifixion of the old man, the destruction of the body of sin, the cleansing of the heart with the precious blood of Jesus from all sin, and the abiding and keeping power of the Holy Spirit. And we humbly ask this in the name of thy Son, our Lord and Saviour Jesus Christ. Amen.

www.ingramcontent.com/pod-product-compliance
Lightning Source LLC
Chambersburg PA
CBHW031355040426
42444CB00005B/303